# THE CHURCH
## *and the*
# RACIAL DIVIDE

*Finding Unity in the Race-Transcending Gospel*

# Trevor Atwood

GENERAL EDITORS

## Daniel Darling and Trillia Newbell

LifeWay Press®
Nashville, Tennessee

# Editorial Team

Reid Patton
*Content Editor*

Susan Hill
*Production Editor*

Jon Rodda
*Art Director*

Joel Polk
*Editorial Team Leader*

Brian Daniel
*Manager, Short-Term Disicpleship*

Michael Kelley
*Director, Discipleship and Groups Ministry*

Ben Mandrell
*President, LifeWay Christian Resources*

Published by LifeWay Press® • © 2019 ERLC

No part of this book may be reproduced or transmitted in any form or by any means, electronic or mechanical, including photocopying and recording, or by any information storage or retrieval system, except as may be expressly permitted in writing by the publisher. Requests for permission should be addressed in writing to LifeWay Press®; One LifeWay Plaza; Nashville, TN 37234.

ISBN 9781535988162 • Item 005820932

Dewey decimal classification: 261.8
Subject headings: CHURCH AND RACE RELATIONS / POPULAR CULTURE / CHRISTIANITY

Unless otherwise noted, all Scripture quotations are taken from the Christian Standard Bible®, Copyright © 2017 by Holman Bible Publishers. Used by permission. Christian Standard Bible® and CSB® are federally registered trademarks of Holman Bible Publishers.

To order additional copies of this resource, write to LifeWay Resources Customer Service; One LifeWay Plaza; Nashville, TN 37234; fax 615-251-5933; call toll free 800-458-2772; or order online at LifeWay.com; or email orderentry@lifeway.com.

PHOTO CREDITS Page 13: © Alabama Department of Archives and History. Donated by Alabama Media Group. Photo by Tom Self, Birmingham News. Page 31: © Kickstand/iStock Photo. Page 45: © Henri Cartier-Bresson/Magnum Photos. Page 73; © Everett/CSU Archives. Page 89: © Equal Justice Initiative

Printed in the United States of America

Groups Ministry Publishing • LifeWay Resources • One LifeWay Plaza • Nashville, TN 37234

# Contents

# About the Authors

**DANIEL DARLING**, General Editor, is the Vice President for Communications for the ERLC. He is a columnist for Homelife and is a regular contributor to Facts and Trends, Made to Flourish, and In Touch. Dan's work has appeared in USAToday, CNN, Washington Post, Christianity Today, and The Gospel Coalition. Daniel is the host of The Way Home Podcast and an associate pastor at Green Hill Church in Mt. Juliet, Tenn. He is the author of several books, including *The Original Jesus* and *The Dignity Revolution*.

**TRILLIA NEWBELL,** General Editor, is the Director of Community Outreach for the Ethics and Religious Liberty Commission of the SBC. She is the author of *Sacred Endurance: Finding Grace and Strength for a Lasting Faith, If God is For Us: a 6-week Bible study on Romans 8, Fear and Faith: Finding the Peace Your Heart Craves , United: Captured by God's Vision for Diversity*, and the children's book, *God's Very Good Idea: A True Story of God's Delightfully Different Family.* You can find her at trillianewbell.com.

**TREVOR ATWOOD,** Author, graduated from Middle Tennessee State University and then proceeded to get his Master of Divinity at Southeastern Baptist Theological Seminary in Wake Forest, NC. He completed the Summit Network Church Planting Residency at the Summit Church in Durham, NC, which led him to plant City Church in Murfreesboro. Trevor has been married to his wife Keva for 20 years, and they have three boys together: Micah, Isaac, and Simon.

# About the ERLC

The Ethics & Religious Liberty Commission is an entity of the Southern Baptist Convention. The ERLC is dedicated to engaging the culture with the gospel of Jesus Christ and speaking to issues in the public square for the protection of religious liberty and human flourishing. Our vision can be summed up in three words: kingdom, culture, and mission.

Since its inception, the ERLC has been defined around a holistic vision of the kingdom of God, leading the culture to change within the church itself and then as the church addresses the world.

## The Mission of the ERLC

The Ethics & Religious Liberty Commission exists to assist the churches by helping them understand the moral demands of the gospel, apply Christian principles to moral and social problems and questions of public policy, and to promote religious liberty in cooperation with the churches and other Southern Baptist entities.

# How to Use this Study

*This Bible-study book includes six weeks of content for group and personal study.*

## Group Sessions

Regardless of what day of the week your group meets, each week of content begins with the group session. Each group session uses the following format to facilitate simple yet meaningful interaction among group members, with God's Word, and with the video teaching.

**START.** This section includes questions to get the conversation started and to introduce the video teaching.

**DISCUSS.** This section includes questions and statements that guide the group to respond to the biblical teaching in the video sessions and to explore relevant Bible passages.

**ENGAGE.** This section helps us apply the truths from the video teaching and make steps towards action.

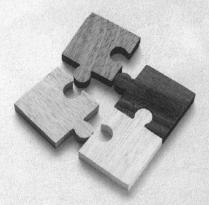

# Personal Study

Each week provides three days of Bible study and learning activities for individual engagement between group sessions. The personal study revisits stories, Scriptures, and themes introduced in the video teaching so that participants can understand and apply them on a personal level.

Each personal study includes the following three sections.

### RENEWED THINKING.

This section provides Biblical teaching meant to deepen and further clarify your understanding of the week's topic. Here you will find a substantial interaction with relevant Scriptures passages to help you think biblically.

### GOSPEL APPLICATION.

Building on the Renewed Thinking section, this section is meant to help you process what you are learning and should be transforming the way you live. This section is designed to deepen your compassion and empathy towards others.

### FAITH IN ACTION.

This section closes out the week's teaching and leaves you with practical ways to begin engaging the world around you with what you are learning.

Broken Mirrors and
Poor Reflections

## THE CHURCH
### *and the*
## RACIAL DIVIDE

**THINK**
How does the gospel speak
to issues of race?

WEEK 1     *Finding Unity in the Race-Transcending Gospel*     VOLUME I

# Imago Dei

> "May men learn to replace bitterness
> and violence with love and understanding."

| *Renewed Thinking* | *Gospel Application* | *Faith in Action* |
|---|---|---|
| *Four Girls Killed in Church Bombing* | **The Image of God Marred by Sin.** | We must be people of compassion and justice. |
| **GENESIS 1:27 —** *Man Created in God's Image* | **Opening Blind Eyes to the Sin of Racism** | |
| | **Racial Unity Rooted in the Gospel** | |

## Start

**Welcome to Session 1 of *The Church and the Racial Divide*.
Use these questions to open the group session.**

Ask group members to introduce themselves by
sharing names, and background information.

What excites you about this study? What is
one thing you're hoping to learn?

We're here together to talk openly and honestly about what the Bible says about race, ethnicity, and how the gospel of Jesus Christ reconciles us to diverse brothers and sisters in one family. In the coming weeks, let's commit to speak honestly, but with love and gentleness, recognizing that God loves the truth as well as a repentant heart.

When discussing an important topic like race, why must we assume
the best in others and give one another the benefit of the doubt?

Before watching this week's video teaching, pray for your group to engage with openness to the Scripture and sensitivity to the leading of the Holy Spirit. Ask God to work in your heart, challenge your assumptions, and eliminate defensiveness. Pray for confession, repentance, faith, hope, and love to be the markers of this group.

## *Discuss*

In the video, Dan Darling pointed out that in Genesis 2:7 God, "breathed the breath of life" into the first human. This set humans apart from all other created things. This means all people equally bear God's image and are different from all of creation, simply because we are human.

**What does the image of God have to do with our thoughts about race and ethnicity?**

**How does the image of God speak to issues like abortion, mental or physical disability, or euthanasia?**

**What are some of the ways humans are uniquely gifted by God to be like Him?**

The video mentioned historical atrocities of genocide and racism—like the Holocaust, apartheid, and slavery. Many of the people that participated in those evils were ordinary people we'd consider good and civil. Some of them even claimed to be Christians.

**How should the Bible's teaching on the image of God shape the way we think about race?**

Many today tend to view racism as a sin of the past that's not part of who we are as a country, people, or church today. Yet, those in the past did not view themselves as racist either. Racism happens any time we judge a person based on skin color or culture. Is there a people group that we might not understand or might avoid? What assumptions do we make about folks who don't look like us? How can the Bible's teaching about the image of God change our perspective? All of us have work to do. The goal of this study is to help you along in that process.

**Dan said, "Racism is sin in two ways. It demeans both the glory of God and the gospel of God." What did he mean? What is an example of each?**

**Other than outright racism, what are common ways we don't see the image of God in others around us?**

To demean another human being based on race is to demean and deny the image of God in them, which is an assault on God's glory. Additionally, because the gospel reconciles all people to God, racism is also anti-gospel. The church is supposed to be a model of the multiethnic kingdom of God.

**Think about your church family. How can you contribute to a multiethnic kingdom oriented culture there?**

**What are some ways a church can show their community they value all people?**

## Engage

**OVER THE NEXT WEEK CONSIDER THESE THINGS IN LIGHT OF WHAT WE'VE STUDIED TOGETHER.**

**Identify groups of people you tend to lump together and only consider as one big group. For example: liberal, conservative, men, women, immigrant, black, white, Asian, Latino, etc. What are some unhelpful assumptions you make about these categories?**

**Pay close attention to your environment, media intake, and relationships. Are the people you live near and interact with mostly the same as you or different than you?**

**We all have inherent biases and assumptions. Changing these assumptions must begin with prayer. Pray for God to show you the humanity in individuals of that group.**

*Pray for God to bring people into your life that are unlike you. Ask Him for an opportunity to recognize that person's humanity and learn from them. Write out your prayer in the space below.*

# What Went Wrong?

**When do you first remember becoming aware of the tensions around race and ethnicity? What about this episode stuck out to you?**

On Sunday, September 15, 1963, in Birmingham, Alabama, in a church full of stained glass windows, teenagers were excited about the day's events. They were preparing to lead a congregation in worship for the annual "Youth Sunday."

Early that morning, four members of the Ku Klux Klan planted a box of dynamite under the steps of the 16th Street Baptist Church. They set a timer to go off at 10:22 a.m. The boys and girls gathered for Sunday School wearing freshly pressed shirts and dresses. In a matter of minutes, their clothes would be soiled with blood, ash, rubble, and tears.

Four little girls were killed in the blast.

*Addie Mae Collins was fourteen.*

*Denise McNair was eleven.*

*Cynthia Wesley was fourteen.*

*Carole Robertson was fourteen.*

They were murdered because their skin was black.

Every stained glass window in the church was blown out that day except one. The unshattered window is called, "The Good Shepherd," which depicts Jesus knocking at a door. The explosion blew out Jesus' face while leaving the rest of the picture intact. The stained-glass picture of the perfect image of God—now broken.

When we see terrible atrocities, we naturally want to ask, "What went wrong?" To figure that out, let's start at the beginning—literally, in Genesis 1.

A stained glass window bears testament to a bomb's damage; Sixteenth Street Baptist Church, September 15, 1963. Tom Self

# Created to Image God

**READ GENESIS 1:24–27**

**What does it mean to be made in the image of God? (vv. 26-27)**

**READ GENESIS 2:7**

**What distinguishes man from the rest of the created order?**

**What do the distinctions between man and the rest of creation teach us about what it means to bear God's image?**

Being made in the image of God means that human beings are like God in a way that the rest of the created order is not. When God created other living things—insects, fish, animals, and plants—He created them according to "their kinds" (v. 24). But God broke that pattern when He created humans. Only human beings are made in the image of God. He didn't create a new "kind" or a new pattern—He used Himself as the pattern. He cut humans from His cloth. He created the rest of the world with a verbal command; He created mankind with the breath of His nostrils and shaped Adam with His hands (2:7). It was personal and intimate. All human beings were created through an intimate act initiated by a loving God and have been imbued with purpose and value by their Creator.

**READ GENESIS 1:28–30.**

**What work did God give the man in the garden? What does that work teach us about what it means to image God?**

God also gave us work—to "be fruitful and multiply" to "fill the earth" and "subdue it" to "rule" and "have dominion"—to assure that the rest of the earth is filled with image-bearers that bring honor and glory to God. We work as God works.

**Now that we have established what the image of God is, what makes God different from creatures made in His image? How is God unlike us?**

To be made in the image of God means that we are, by definition—not God. God is infinite; we are finite. He is all-knowing; we learn everything we know. We are dependent on God's provision. We need God; He doesn't need us. We are images of God— not God.

And yet, we are made in the image of God. That means we communicate God's existence and His love to the world. We image God when we create. Like God, we think, have dominion, and execute justice and mercy. We are fruitful, and we multiply, filling the world with image-bearers who, like us, are different and better than the rest of creation. Yet, inside of all of us lurks a dangerous deception—a voice that tells us we are more than the image of God. The voice tells us we are gods. We first heard this voice back in the garden.

# The Image Assaulted

**READ GENESIS 3:1–6**
**What lie did Satan tell the man and woman? How did following the lie actually make the man and woman less like God?**

Though human beings were created to image God, the serpent pitched an alternative idea. He said humans shouldn't be dependent on God and rule creation. Rather, humans should be dependent on creation and rule God.

This lie takes many forms: "Eat the fruit. Let your instincts and desires guide you. Do what you feel! Be your authentic self! Take and eat! Decide for yourself what is good and evil. Let the tree make you wise. Become strong and compete. Don't image God—be God." But our attempt to become more like God only results in physical and spiritual death.

**Where do you see this same lie at work in our
culture today? What are the effects?**

What happened next? Very simply, the curse of separation and death began. Man and woman hid from each other and God, blamed one another, and were cast out of the garden. Their fellowship with God was broken. In the next chapter, one of Adam and Eve's sons murdered his brother, three chapters later, sin has so engulfed the earth, and the image of God is so assaulted that God brings a flood and starts over.

**How is the strife and discord we experience
today related to that day in the garden?**

# Four Little Girls, Four Broken Men, and the Good Shepherd

Let's go back to 16th Street Baptist Church in 1963 Birmingham to connect these biblical dots to the faces of those children and that Good Shepherd.

**What makes racism sinful?**

**What must one deny about another person made in the image of God to embrace racial superiority?**

The men that set that bomb were separated from God. They wanted to keep humans, particularly black humans, separate from them. In order to do that, they denied their full humanity on the basis of skin color. They refused to believe the image of God, the dignity and beauty of our Creator, was present in men, women, boys, and girls meeting at 16th Street Baptist Church. The didn't see their humanity.

The sin of racism is a denial of the image of God. Racism puts human beings in the place of God and seeks to have dominion over them. It seeks to consume, instead of cultivating. It listens to the voice of the serpent and hides from God. Racism, in every form, is evil. It's comforting to tell ourselves racism is a thing of the past that we're not involved in today. It's comforting—but misleading.

Unfortunately, racism is alive and well. If our first thought is, "I don't see it," then this Bible study was written for you. Our aim is to approach the Word of God, even if it unsettles us and causes us to repent and mourn over our sin so we can be sanctified. Then the gospel will leave us hopeful, changed, and ready for action

Ultimately, this Bible study is for all of us—to see the glory of God's design, the amazing grace bestowed upon all who believe, and the blood-bought unity Jesus brings to all people regardless of who we are, what color our skin is, or what culture we came from.

**READ EPHESIANS 2:14.**

**How has Jesus broken down the walls of hostility between you and people who are different from you, racially or otherwise?**

---

*Take time and pray, asking God to search your heart and reveal to you hidden biases and prejudices. Invite Him to expose your heart and pray that you would be willing to accept His affliction and corrections.*

# An Ancient Problem

**READ GENESIS 3:15–20**

When the first man and woman distrusted God and trampled His image, things got ugly. Their sin resulted in a curse, separation, and death. Still, in the middle of all that darkness, there was a light shining. Adam resumed his God-given role as a "namer," and he called his wife, "Eve—the mother of the living," which seems strange. Because just before God delivered the curse, Adam blamed his wife, and now he's praising her.

Adam was separated from Eve with a fig leaf. Now, he is drawing closer and becoming one again (4:1). The Scripture raises a curious question—why does the man bless the woman with this name? Why not curse her? Why not call her "mother of death" or "tool of the serpent?" (Not that Adam doesn't bear as much or more responsibility than Eve for his role in this original sin, but remember, he's already been blaming).

The answer is in Genesis 3:15.

**What did God promise to do through Eve?**

**God acts graciously towards us despite our open rebellion.**
**What does this teach us about the character of God?**

Genesis 3:15 has been called the "protoevangelion." It means "first gospel." God made a promise to crush the head of the serpent—the source of the great lie that humans could be gods and should act like beasts. But it would come at a price. The seed of the woman, this child who would end the serpent's lie, would suffer. His heel would be bruised.

Adam named Eve "mother of the living" because of God's promise to deliver salvation from the curse through Eve's offspring—a son of man who would suffer to heal the hurts of humanity. The image of God marred by sin would be restored in a perfect Son. Of course, this promise is realized in God's true son, the Son of Man, Jesus Christ. Jesus would become the offspring of the woman who would crush the heel of the serpent to heal those to whom the serpent lied.

**READ ROMANS 5:15–18**

**How do Jesus' death and resurrection heal the effects of Adam's sin?**

We read Romans 5 in light of Genesis 3:15. The promise God gave to Adam and Eve was fulfilled in Jesus. At the cross, the curse of sin was broken and reversed. The grace of Jesus canceled the trespass in the garden. The gospel radically transforms from the inside out and impacts every aspect of our lives. The cross restores image-bearers to their image-bearing work.

# A Gospel Solution

In the early church, grace brought Jews and Gentiles together in one community. Issues abounded as they knit these two separate communities together into one family of God. Let's take a look at how this gospel applies to the way we look at different races, cultures, and ethnicities.

**READ EPHESIANS 2:8–20 AND GALATIANS 2:11–20**

**How did Paul apply the gospel to racial divides
(Jew and Gentile) in the first century?**

**Why would Paul make an appeal through the gospel
instead of saying something more straightforward,
such as, "Racism is wrong. You shouldn't do it!"?**

All people, regardless of their genetic or ethnic makeup, were at one time outside of the family of God. We were "foreigners to the covenants of promise" (Eph. 2:12). But we, who were once foreigners, have been brought near to God and made part of His family. What's more, God's family is comprised of people from every ethnicity and language (Matt. 24:14; 28:18–20; Rev. 5:9–10). Paul rooted his call to racial unity in the gospel because racism is a sin issue, and the gospel is the only message in the world that can fully deal with sin. Where sin divides and pits image-bearers against each other, the gospel brings us together.

**How should the gospel shape the way you deal
with racism in the world around you?**

**Consider how you think about and treat people of different
ethnicities. How might your heart be out of line with the gospel?**

# Historical Heart Check

Now, let's think historically. Unfortunately, history is littered with example of racial sin and injustice—the 1960s American South, Nazi Germany in the 1940s, Japanese internment camps, South African apartheid, the Middle Passage in the 18th century, Rwanda in 1994, the first-century Jews and Gentiles, and the slaughter of Native Americans in 17th century—to name only a few examples. For these atrocities to have occurred, people had to turn a blind eye towards the sin of racism. Even more, unfortunately, many Bible-believing churchgoers were complicit in these historical episodes, both in their participation and their silence.

As Galatians 2 shows us, there's no room for God's people to remain dispassionate or uninvolved when sin is in our midst. We must be people of compassion and justice.

**Why must we not see these as events in the distant past with no lesson for the church today?**

**What steps can you take to uphold the inherent value and worth of all people?**

**Write down four ways that "the image of God" should affect the way we see people of different ethnicities.**

*Close your time by praying for God to continue to reveal areas where you have considered yourself superior to others based on your race or ethnicity. Ask God to allow you to see all people as He does, as made in His image and of inestimable worth and value.*

# Hear from God and One Another

The book of James is full of proverbial wisdom that takes many of the ideas we find in the New Testament and provides practical wisdom so it can be applied to our lives. So as we are seeking to put our faith in action, there's no better place to look. This short book has much to teach us about what it means to value people made in the image of God

### READ JAMES 1:19–25; 2:14–20

When we don't see the value in other people, we stop listening to what they have to say. Much of the heartache around issues of race could be abated if we would stop and take the time to listen to one another. Doing this allows us to hear both from God and one another.

Furthermore, our faith should extend beyond simply hearing into the realm of doing. Action proves that our faith is genuine. It shows that we have been changed by God. Taken together, our words and our deeds outwardly demonstrate our internal faith.

**How have I used my words to dehumanize people
of other races, ethnicities, or cultures?**

**How have I neglected to defend and care for people of other races?**

We must recognize that our ill-timed and insensitive words are a source of great pain and hardship for others. James continues to give wisdom about our words.

# Tame Your Tongue

### READ JAMES 3:7–18; 4:1–10

In chapter three, James gives us Genesis 1–3 language. He says that mankind has tamed every kind of animal (part of the command in Genesis 1–2), but we can't tame the tongue. Our words are full of deadly poison—like a serpent.

And what do we do with those poisonous words? We curse humans made in God's image. Just like the venomous lie from the serpent led to a curse of God's image-bearers, so the way we talk about other humans is either life-giving or demonic (3:15,17).

Chapter four starts with the sort of hostility that we found in the curse—hostility toward God and fellow humanity. The kind of hostility that manifested itself in Genesis 4 onward.

So, how should we respond? Humble ourselves, and God will provide grace (Jas. 4:6). Weep for sin. Mourn for the dehumanization of God's image-bearers. Set yourself apart by admitting the ways you have seen sin hurt others, and for the times you have participated in it. Don't defend yourself. Humble yourself under God, and you will be exalted. Not as God, but as the image of God.

So let's spend the rest of this session considering how God is calling us to obey His Word.

**What's your first reaction to an act of violence against a person of a different race than your own? What can you glean from that?**

**How can you place yourself in proximity to other ethnicities so you can learn from them and see the image of God in them?**

The gospel pulls us toward God and each other. What are
a few simple ways you can change daily or weekly habits
to put yourself in proximity to and have conversations
with other image-bearers of a different ethnicity?

Are your friendships as diverse as your community? If not, why not?

What is one simple step you can take this week to expand
your friendships (reach out to a neighbor, strike up a
conversation at a kid's ballgame, at the store, etc)?

With whom can you share about what you
learned during this week's study?

| Seperate but Equal vs. Unified and Unique | THE CHURCH *and the* RACIAL DIVIDE | **THINK** What is the difference between uniformity and unity? |
| --- | --- | --- |

WEEK 2      *Finding Unity in the Race-Transcending Gospel*      VOLUME II

# God's Heart for All People

## "The goal is not uniformity, but unity."
### — Dr. Walter Strickland

| *Renewed Thinking* | *Gospel Application* | *Faith In Action* |
| --- | --- | --- |
| A Commission to the Nations | God wants people from every race to be saved. | I *Pray* |
| **Brown v. Board of Education** | | II *Read* |
| **EPHESIANS 2:10–17** | | III *Learn From Others* |

**Review**

Welcome to Session 2. Use these questions to open the group session.

Last week you spent some time in individual study about what it means to be made in God's image.

**What was an idea from Scripture that impacted
you about the image of God?**

**How might God be asking you to change or grow? What
is one step you're taking based on last week's study?**

**Start**

**What is something you have learned by spending time with
someone who comes from a different culture than your own?**

Last week we learned that people of every race, culture, and ethnicity equally bear the image of God. Because of this glorious truth, we can learn about God through our relationships with other people. This week, we're going to learn about God's heart for all ethnicities.

**BEFORE WATCHING THE VIDEO, SPEND A FEW MINUTES IN PRAYER.**

*Ask the Spirit to help your group to be open and honest and ready to listen.
Thank God for giving us the Scriptures that reveals His heart to us.*

Video sessions available at LifeWay.com/thechurchandtheracialdivide or with a subscription to SmallGroup.com

## Discuss

### READ GENESIS 11:1–9

**Why did God divide people with language barriers and
scatter them apart from each other geographically?**

### READ GENESIS 12:1–3

**What happens in these verses? How do you see God
bringing back together what was separated at Babel?**

In Genesis 11, the prideful sin of humanity puts them under a curse of division. Men and women used their unity to try and climb to God's rightful place, so God divided them into different language groups. Yet, in Genesis 12, God promised to unite all people through the blessing given to one man—Abraham. Through Abraham, God created one people who were meant to show the world what it means to live in a relationship with Him. The church plays a pivotal role in this ongoing mission.

### READ MATTHEW 28:19–20

**What role does the church play in God's plan to
unite all people to Himself? Why is it sinful to refuse
to engage people of different ethnicities?**

### READ EPHESIANS 2:10–17

Dr. Strickland pointed out that believing the gospel prepared the church to reconcile two ethnic groups who were at odds with each other. Pursuing the "good works" God has prepared for us (v. 10) means, in part, pursuing unity across ethnic dividing lines.

**Why is division on the basis of ethnicity against
the gospel? Why do we tolerate it?**

Dr. Strickland also said, "The goal is not uniformity, but unity."

**What is the difference between uniformity and unity?
How might you have unity without uniformity?**

**What are some of the most common fears in becoming a local church, united in Christ, but with diverse races, cultures, and backgrounds?**

### Engage

Let's discuss ways we can practice Dr. Strickland's advice to develop God's heart for all people.

## INCARNATION (OR SIMPLY BEING PRESENT)

Jesus demonstrated His care for us by taking on flesh and coming to be with us. Similarly, we can practice incarnational ministry by spending intentional time with people showing them we are present and that we care.

**Who is a person/people of a different ethnicity that you can invite to lunch or coffee?**

## ELEVATING KINGDOM IDENTITY

**Consider the identities you are most protective of (race, sports team, political affiliation, your church, family role, job, etc). Which one is most prone to replace your identity as a Christ-follower, and why?**

## LEARNING FROM OTHER CULTURES

Learning about other cultures helps you appreciate the gifts they bring to the world.

**Are there some documentaries or shows you could watch as a family to learn about other cultures? Is there anywhere you could travel together, even in your own town?**

**What might it look like to devote your dinner conversations a couple of times a week to discussing something you've learned from another culture?**

> *End today's session in a time of confession to God about self-centered and ethnic-centered thinking. Then, ask God to give you a heart like His for all nations.*

# Separate But Not Equal

In 1896, the Plessy v. Ferguson Supreme Court decision allowed states to legally separate blacks and whites as long as "equal" accommodations were provided for both races. The legal precedent was known as "separate but equal."

In 1954, Plessy v Ferguson was overturned by another Supreme Court case—Brown v. Board of Education. This decision called for schools, restaurants, swimming pools, community centers, and other public spaces to integrate the races. Of course, having a law tell you something is very different than having the heart to do it. Desegregation, particularly in the southern states, didn't happen overnight. It was heavily resisted, and many sought to find loopholes that would allow it to continue—because their heart was opposed to the law.

Sadly, the Bible was used to provide reasons for "separate but equal," as if God's heart was to elevate one race over another or to keep races separate. This week, we'll look at what God reveals in Scripture about his heart for all races and what that means for how we think about race.

### READ ACTS 17:24–29 & REVELATION 7:9–10
**What do these passages teach about God's heart for all races?**

Both the origin and the destination of all ethnicities is together with God. When Paul addressed the philosophers in Athens, he noted that every race came from the first man—Adam, and that it's by God's design that those races live to know God.

In Revelation, John tells us that the endpoint of every tribe, tongue, and nation is together, praising the God that rescued them. Think about that. There are only two scenes of absolute perfection and peace in the Bible; the beginning and the end. All races are present in both. Their origin is in the garden of Eden with Adam. Their destination is the new Jerusalem with God.

**How should seeing the diversity around the throne room
of God shape how we think about ethnicity today?**

Separate but not equal water
fountains under segregation.
Levine Museum of the New South.
Kickstand/iStock Photo

# STATE — THE TOPEKA — JOURNAL

AN INDEPENDENT NEWSPAPER

**Home Edition**

By Stauffer Publications, Inc.

Topeka, Kansas, Monday, May 17, 1954 — Twenty-four Pages

Official City Paper

**FIVE CENTS**

# SCHOOL SEGREGATION BANNED

## Turnpike Bonds Authorized So Suit Can Start

### Supreme Court Will Clear Legal Air in Friendly Action

## Supreme Court Refutes Doctrine of Separate but Equal Education

### High Tribunal Fails to Specify When Practice of Dual Schools Must Be Dropped by States

Washington, May 17 (AP)—The Supreme court ruled unanimously Monday that segregation of Negro and white students in public schools is unconstitutional. But it asked it will hear further arguments this fall on how and when to end the practice.

*Laying Track at the Fairgrounds for 'Cyrus Holliday'*

This special crew from the Santa Fe railroad was hard at work Monday morning putting down a 300-foot strip of track on which the 1880 Cyrus K. Holliday locomotive and one car will chug into the Centennial pageant. The operation was almost identical to the type of work done in early days to move the tracks across native prairie—rough-hewn ties, light rail and trucks laid directly to bare earth.

### Court Ruling Hailed

## Segregation Already Ending Here, Say School Officials

Jacob A. Dickinson, president of the Topeka Board of Education, hailed the Supreme court's segregation ruling Monday as "in the finest spirit of the law and true democracy."

### Rainfall Spread

The Topeka State Journal, May 17, 1954

In the New Testament, when you read the English word "nations," it doesn't mean geographic or political nations, as we typically understand the word. The Greek word behind it is "ethnos," where we get our word "ethnicity." So when you see the word "nations," the biblical authors are usually referring to ethnicities.

# A Commission to the Nations

### READ MATTHEW 28:18–20 & ACTS 1:8

When Jesus commissioned the first Christians, He sent them out with a task to be His witnesses in all the earth and make disciples of all nations (or ethnicities). God's desire is not simply that different races exist peacefully. His desire is not just for people from different races to be nice to each other. Rather, God's heart is for people from every tribe, tongue, and nation be saved. And He promises that He is going to use His church, made up of people from every ethnicity, to reach them. If the heart of God is to be the heart of the church, the church must have God's vision for the togetherness of all ethnicities worshiping Him together.

### What are the implications of Jesus' commands?

### READ MARK 11:15–17

### What led Jesus to overturn the tables in the temple?

The temple in Jerusalem had different layers of accessibility. The inner sections of the temple could only be accessed by Jews, but the outer porch was intended to be a place that even the Gentiles could come to pray and seek God. When Jesus entered the temple, all the space designed to give the Gentiles a venue to connect to God was instead filled with people trying to sell goods for profit. Jesus was not happy about it.

The temple was meant to bring the nations together, not drive them apart. It was meant to show God's glory to all the peoples of the world. Jesus designed the church to be a new and better temple that reflects God's glory to all the nations of the earth (see 1 Pet. 2:5). God's desire is for people of all ethnicities to be together in one body. We have no reason to separate what God knit together through the blood of His Son.

**Jesus overturned the tables to restore the temple to it's intended function. How does pursuing a multiethnic church restore the church to its intended purpose?**

**How can you contribute to your local church becoming a place that welcomes people of all backgrounds so that they can encounter the life-changing message of the gospel?**

**Do you think your heart is in step with God's heart for all ethnicities? Why or why not?**

*End today with a prayer of confession and repentance and ask God to align your heart with His.*

# The Gospel for All People

It's impossible to talk about God's heart without talking about salvation. God doesn't just want all races to exist; He wants people from every race to be saved.

**READ 1 TIMOTHY 2:1–7**

**How many times does Paul emphasize that the gospel is for "all" people in these verses?**

**Why do you think Paul says that he was appointed as a "teacher of the Gentiles" in the same section he addressed God's desire that all people are saved?**

In these verses, Paul summarized the gospel—that Jesus is the one mediator between God and humanity. There isn't a different mediator for each race. There isn't one for Jews and one for Gentiles. There isn't a Jesus for hispanic people and another for black people and another for white people. Jesus gave Himself as a ransom for all people.

**READ 1 TIMOTHY 2:8**

Notice the "therefore" in v. 8 that follows Paul's summation of the gospel in verses 5–6. In other words, Paul is saying, "since Jesus gave himself as a ransom for all, *therefore* men everywhere should pray without anger or argument."

**Why should a gospel for all people produce unified prayer for people everywhere?**

Later in Paul's letter to Timothy, he summarized the gospel again in what was probably an early hymn of the church.

**READ 1 TIMOTHY 3:16**

**Why would Paul include "preached among the nations (ethnos) and believed in the world" in this gospel summary?**

**Does Paul seem to think about race as a "gospel issue"? Why or why not?**

**What does the church gain as people of all nations come to faith in Jesus?**

**What would change about the character of God if He didn't care about "all peoples?"**

## AT THE END OF TODAY'S STUDY, EVALUATE THE WAY YOU THINK AND TALK ABOUT RACE.

Social media outlets tend to be the spaces where many people are most vocal with their thoughts about issues of race. When a racially-charged news story, book, or movie comes out, people often say things they wouldn't say to a person's face by way of a social media post. In the context of a passage about God's heart for all people, Paul says that Christians should aim to lead a tranquil and quiet life in all godliness and dignity without anger or arguing (1 Thess. 4:11).

**Think about your social media use. If you post about racially charged issues, do your posts promote unity, prayer, holiness, godliness, and dignity?**

**Does your commentary or silence on issues of race (online or in-person) make it harder or easier for a person to hear the gospel come from your mouth? How so?**

**What do the jokes you accept and laugh at communicate about your feelings towards other ethnicities?**

Tomorrow, you'll read about some steps you can take to help move your heart closer to God's heart on issues of race in our culture. For now, will you ask God to give you a heart like His for all nations?

# Look Around You

**READ HEBREWS 10:16 & 1 CORINTHIANS 2:16**

Scripture is clear that we are to have the "mind of Christ" and that God wants our heart's desires synced to His. This week, you have seen that God's heart is for the salvation of all ethnicities and that He is using His church to accomplish that mission.

**Use your smartphone to download the app "IMB Pray."**

This app will give you different people groups around the world to pray for. As you pray for those groups, you'll also learn a little about the people. Use this app in your daily prayer time. Prayer is foundational to molding your heart to be like God's.

**What people group is today's prayer about?**

**If you used this app five days a week and intentionally prayed for a people group, how might God work in you and through your prayers?**

Is there a people group you are already inclined to pray for? If so, who? Write out a prayer for them below.

Go to namb.net/compassion. Click on the link for Refugees and Internationals. Browse some of the ways that you can be a help to people from other nations who may live around you.

Will you contact a pastor in your church and ask if there is anything your church is already doing to help refugees? If not, would you volunteer to put something together?

Go to City-Data.com. Look up your city and look at racial demographic information around your house and church.

Do the people that you invite into your home match the demographics around you? Why or why not?

Does your church reflect the demographics of the neighborhood it is located in? Why or why not?

Are there other churches in the area that do reflect the demographic? Would you be willing to talk with one of those church leaders about how they are reaching people in your area?

# Learn from Others

One of the ways we can develop God's heart for all people is to interact with the experiences of others. Taking the time to see the world from someone else's viewpoint broadens our horizons and deepens our understanding. Here are a few suggestions.

**Who in your church is doing ministry among ethnic minorities? Consider asking them to meet with you and share what they do and what motivates them to do it?**

**Spend some time researching Christian and non-Christian organizations that work with refugee populations. What did you learn about the people these organizations serve and why?**

**Could you write to or have a conversation with a missionary who has served in another country? What motivated them to leave home and serve others?**

**What is one simple thing you could do this week to establish a relationship with someone who doesn't look like you?**

Resist the Urge To
Be Color-Blind

THE CHURCH
*and the*
RACIAL DIVIDE

THINK
What does unity in
suffering look like?

WEEK 3      *Finding Unity in the Race-Transcending Gospel*      VOLUME III

# Breaking Down the Walls

## The gospel is transcending because the gospel is the ultimate unifier.

| *Renewed Thinking* | *Gospel Application* | *Faith in Action* |
| --- | --- | --- |

*Your suffering is my suffering.*

—

**Let them come to Berlin!**
**—JFK**

## Tearing Down Walls

EPHESIANS 2:19–21
—

**HEBREWS 4:15**
—
Listen & Empathize
—

*In our call to live as Christ lived, we need to seek to sympathize with one another.*

## *Review*

Welcome to Session 3. Use these questions to open the group session.

During last week's sessions, you studied about God's heart for all the nations.

**In response to the Faith In Action session, did anyone
look up the demographics of the area of town you live
in? What did you learn from that information?**

**What are ways that you believe God might be calling you to change
or grow? What steps might you take to implement that change?**

## *Start*

Think about all the homes that you've lived in during your life—dorm rooms, apartments, neighborhoods, or rural areas. If you lived in a neighborhood, you might have had a privacy fence. If you lived in a dorm or apartment, you might have had a common area. It's a pretty common practice to move away from "common area" living and move toward "privacy fence" living. Open the garage. Close the garage. Hang out in the back yard where we are protected from one another by a fence. Not many of us do life anymore in the front yard or in common areas.

**Why do we gravitate towards privacy? How do walls
and fences keep us from enjoying our neighbors?**

**Why do we avoid "common area" living?**

This week, the Scripture is going to help us see walls that go up between races and how Christ moves in us to live with other ethnicities in a "common area."

**BEFORE WATCHING THE VIDEO, SPEND A FEW MINUTES IN PRAYER.**

> *Pray for God to reveal the walls we've put up and for
> the Holy Spirit to help us tear them down.*

Video sessions available at LifeWay.com/thechurchandtheracialdivide or with a subscription to SmallGroup.com

*Discuss*

**READ ACTS 11:19–21.**

Because of persecution, the church was scattered. They were sharing the gospel with others, but only with others of their own ethnicity—the Jews. It took the bold men from Cyprus and Cyrene, to break out of the Jewish "backyard" and into the "common area" that included the Greeks.

**Why is it difficult to be the person to make the first move in starting a relationship or sharing the gospel with someone?**

**READ EPHESIANS 2:8–14**

Most of us really love that God made the first move toward us to overcome our sin and unite us with Him. What's often harder for us to grasp is that because God united us to Himself, He now calls us to pursue others in need of the gospel. God is calling you out of your private space and into the common area.

**Why is it challenging for us to embrace the truth that God has called us to cross ethnic lines to seek unity in the gospel?**

**Where have you or people you know been resistant to God's call to cross barriers with the gospel?**

**Several times Trillia refers to the gospel as "race-transcending." What does that mean?**

To transcend is to go above or beyond. The gospel is "race transcending" because the gospel is the ultimate unifier. All people are unified both in their need for the gospel and the blessing they receive from it. The gospel drives us to tear dividing walls created by sin. Trillia mentions three ways to tear down walls between races.

1. Resist the urge to be color-blind.
2. Don't show partiality to people because of their race.
3. Replace apathy with empathy.

**How might seeing and acknowledging someone's ethnicity help us to overcome racial barriers?**

How might pretending differences don't exist between ethnicities hurt
others and put walls up that prevent us from spreading the gospel?

What does it communicate about our belief in the
gospel if we show partiality based on race?

How does being empathetic to racial struggles and concerns
(i.e. understanding how brothers and sisters have been treated)
better reflect God's heart in the gospel over apathy?

Where are you most drawn into apathy?

### Engage

Trillia ended with a challenge to evaluate yourself and confess any sin that could
prevent racial harmony. Spend some time over the next week in prayer using the
categories of color-blindness, partiality, and apathy as a guideline.

Pray for the Lord to give you discernment about who you
might need to ask for their forgiveness in these areas—whether
you knowingly or unknowingly sinned against them.

Ask God to reveal how you show partiality for your own race
or against another race. As He reveals it, agree with Him about
it, and thank Him that you are forgiven because of Jesus.

Ask God to show you how you have been apathetic to racially-charged
issues in your city and/or country. Seek an opportunity this week for
you to be empathetic towards someone else's suffering in this category.

*Pray that God would give us grace as we seek to tear down the dividing
walls of hostility between our neighbors and us. Ask that He would
reveal hidden sin and bring fresh conviction where needed.*

# Let Them Come to Berlin!

Following the Allied victory over Nazi Germany in WWII, the city of Berlin was divided into four zones that were each governed by a different allied country—the U.S., France, England, and the Soviet Union. The three areas that were occupied by the US, France, and England were all open. You could freely travel between those zones of Berlin. But the Soviets decided to put up a wall to keep people in because so many of them wanted to leave to escape a communist way of life.

Over time, the barrier grew from barbed wire to trenches, to guard towers with snipers, to an actual concrete wall surrounded by something called a "death zone" where if you stood anywhere close to the wall on the Soviet side, you would be shot.

It became an icon. A symbol of the division between East and West. Between two different political and economic systems. But the thing is, the wall wasn't just an idea or a metaphor; it was a literal wall dividing husbands from wives, parents from children, and friend from friend.

In June of 1961, President John F. Kennedy gave a speech in Berlin.

*"There are many people in the world who really don't understand, or say they don't, what is the great issue between the free world and the Communist world. Let them come to Berlin. There are some who say that communism is the wave of the future. Let them come to Berlin. And there are even a few who say that it is true that communism is an evil system, but it permits us to make economic progress. Let them come to Berlin.*

*While the wall is the most obvious and vivid demonstration of the failures of the Communist system, for all the world to see, we take no satisfaction in it, for it is ...an offense not only against history but an offense against humanity, separating families, dividing husbands and wives and brothers and sisters, and dividing a people who wish to be joined together. Freedom is indivisible, and when one man is enslaved, all are not free. Today, in the world of freedom, the proudest boast is "Ich bin ein Berliner!"*

**— JOHN F. KENNEDY**

Children Playing by the Berlin Wall, 1962. ©Henri Cartier-Bresson/Magnum Photos

President Kennedy was saying, "If anyone thinks communism is the wave of the future, if anyone thinks that communism brings life and flourishing—let them come to Berlin." Look at a city divided. Look at the poverty and oppression. Look at the Berlin wall.

"Let them come to Berlin, and they'll see there is no life, only division and death."

In an effort to identify with the struggle and the hardship of the divided people of Berlin, he said, "I am a Berliner. I am one of you. Your suffering is my suffering and your freedom will be my freedom."

Twenty-six years later, President Ronald Reagan delivered another speech in Berlin, in which he called the leader of the Soviet Union to action. In the six most memorable words from his presidency, President Reagan said, "Mr. Gorbachev, TEAR DOWN THAT WALL!" Two years later, the wall came down. Families reunited. People danced on the broken-down wall that used to divide them. And ultimately, the Soviet Union crumbled. Germany is now a unified country, and Berlin is not East and West—it's just Berlin.

**What are some barriers that divide us today?**

# The Church that Broke the Wall

### READ ACTS 11:19–21

**How was this church established? What do you notice
about the ethnic make-up of this church?**

Two thousand years before Berlin, there was another city separated by a wall. It was called Antioch. But the wall wasn't erected because of political or economic differences. The wall was built to separate different ethnicities

When we think about church, we often think of people we are comfortable with. But the church at Antioch was born out of persecution, not comfort. Antioch was the third-largest city in the Roman Empire. It was diverse but divided. With people from Africa, Asia, Israel, and Mediterranean Europe, Antioch was filled with strangers with different skin colors, ethnicities, and traditions. They ate strange foods, celebrated different holidays, and spoke different languages.

Because of the discord, Antioch was laid out in two sections. And like post-war Berlin, a wall was constructed to keep them separate. At the time of Acts 11, Antioch was divided by more than a wall.

When Christians arrived in Antioch, mostly, they were just looking for their own kind. They were just looking for Jews to convert. But there were a few of them who came from the Island of Cyprus, that knew this gospel was not just for "us." So they started to share the good news about Jesus with the Greeks, too. Suddenly, this multiethnic movement began to sweep through the city. And people in every neighborhood, on both sides of the wall, were hearing the gospel and believing, and then telling it to someone else.

**Imagine you are one of the new converts in this Antioch church.
What would be difficult about starting a new church with so
many different traditions, opinions, and backgrounds?**

**When has the gospel led you to exchange your
preferences to seek unity with another Christian?**

**READ ACTS 11:22–30**

News of this multiethnic church got back to the apostles in Jerusalem, so they sent Barnabas to check it out, and he was blown away by what he discovered. He was looking at people who had nothing in common other than a belief in the resurrected Jesus. He was astounded that they were joining together under the name of Christ and attributed it all to God's grace.

**How does the gospel compel us to work together despite differences?**

# A Multiethnic, Multiplying Church

**READ ACTS 13:1–3**

The Antioch church grew to be not only ethnically and culturally diverse among its members, but their leadership became ethnically diverse as well.

In Acts 13, we get a list of five people who include Asian, African, Jewish, and European descent. Then, the church sent Saul out on his missionary journeys to plant more ethnically diverse churches like the one in Antioch. The church to whom he wrote the New Testament epistles.

As President Kennedy said, "Let them come to Berlin!" to observe the way a dividing wall brings death to a people, Acts 11 says, "Come to Antioch" to see the way the gospel breaks down walls of division and heals a nation.

**Reflect on the way God built the church in Antioch and the fruit of that church. In what ways would a church like this today cause nonbelievers and unchurched folks to look at the church positively?**

**Can you think of a church like this? If so, what does this church communicate about the gospel?**

# Tearing Down the Walls

### READ EPHESIANS 2:1–21

Ephesus was a similar city to Antioch in both its ethnic diversity and the potential problems the church would face from that diversity.

> **Why would Paul spend half of this chapter relating the gospel to unity between Jew and Gentiles? What does that communicate about its importance?**

When reading the Bible, one of the ways we determine what is important to the author—and ultimately, what is important to God—is the amount of space devoted to an idea. The majority of Paul's letters contain large sections devoted to unity between people who normally live separate lives. This was a major issue in the first-century church and continues to be an issue in the twenty-first-century church. Bringing people together is not easy, but we do not have the freedom to disregard the Bible's teaching simply because we find it difficult.

> **If it causes less friction to have single-ethnicity churches, why is it important to pursue diverse churches?**

> **Why should we not avoid pursuing diversity just because it's difficult?**

**Look at verses 13–14 again. How did Jesus both identify with us and tear down the dividing wall between us? What did it cost Jesus to do this?**

Think back to President Kennedy and President Reagan's words in the previous study. President Kennedy impressed upon the people of Berlin that he was with them. President Reagan urged the USSR to break down the wall. In the book of Ephesians, Paul tells us that Jesus both identified with us and removed the wall that divided us.

Jesus came in the flesh. He is one of us. When Christ became human, died on the cross, in His flesh, He broke down the dividing wall of hostility between Jews and the nations. On the cross, Jesus gave His life and opened the door to His church for all to come in.

### REREAD EPHESIANS 2:19–21

**What's the difference in thinking of someone as a stranger and thinking of them as a fellow citizen? How does this translate to our relationship to them?**

Notice how an implication of the gospel changed the way the Jews and Gentiles saw each other. Now, they shouldn't think of the other race as a foreigner or stranger, rather as a fellow citizen or family member.

**What additional metaphor did Paul use in these verses? What does it teach us about what it means to part of the church?**

The end of Ephesians 2 talks about the unified church as the temple of God. Each person is a brick that makes up the dwelling place of God's Spirit. And all of us rest on Jesus Christ, the foundation or cornerstone of this building. Paul uses metaphors of a family and a building to teach that the Church is unified in the gospel despite the other identities (in this chapter, race and ethnicity) that would divide us.

# Co-heirs in the Gospel

**READ EPHESIANS 3:4–6**

**What did Paul mean by the "mystery of Christ?" (v. 4)?**

**What words does Paul use in verse 6 to describe the
Gentiles who were being added to the church?**

As the Gentiles were coming into the church at Ephesus, Paul anticipated that the Jewish members of that church would be uncomfortable. Notice how Paul described their unity in the gospel, the Gentiles were now co-heirs, members, and partners in the gospel. God has taken what men divided and brought it together in the gospel. He has torn down the wall. He is calling you to pursue unity across ethnic diversity.

**Does your church pursue ethnic diversity? Do you? Why or why not?**

**End today with prayer**

*Thank God for bringing together people of different ethnicities and cultures
in a way that displays the mysteries of Christ and the glories of the gospel.
Ask God to use you as a catalyst for unity and diversity in your church.*

# An Acknowledgment

If we desire to break down walls of racial disunity, we first need to understand where the walls are and how they got there. In America, historically, people of color, especially black populations, have been marginalized, first through the Trans-Atlantic slave trade and then Jim Crow laws. And even though we've made much progress on civil rights in this country and things like slavery and Jim Crow are a thing of the past, that doesn't mean the ripple effects of hundreds of years of oppression aren't real and present today.

Decades of systemic injustices have caused hurt, mistrust, and misunderstanding between white and black people. In America, while much progress has been made, there is still much progress to be had. Those in the majority culture, predominantly white populations, still enjoy cultural and social benefits that often still elude people of color.

It's hard for those of us who are in the majority to see this. But to those on the outside, that power and privilege is very obvious. For example, if a white family moves, he can be pretty confident his new neighbors will be neutral or kind to him. He can rest assured that when he does well in school or work, he won't be thought of as a credit to his race. He won't be asked to speak on behalf of all white people, and if he is pulled over by law enforcement, he won't think for one second that it's because of his race.

Those are each examples of the sort of challenges that those in the majority culture may not see happening to brothers and sisters of color, because we operate from a different background, with a different set of experiences.

We shouldn't loathe our background, but it's good to acknowledge the advantages we may have been given. And we should seek to listen and understand the experiences and difficulty that our black brothers and sisters may face. This helps to slowly break down the walls that often divide white and black Christians.

So today, let's focus on two categories of action. Think of these two categories in terms of Ephesians 2:13–14. Christ was "in the flesh" and brought peace when He "tore down the dividing wall of hostility." Likewise, as Christians, we are called to enter into the suffering of others, to listen and understand and work to bring peace.

# In the Flesh Ministry

In our group session this week, we mentioned the incarnation of Jesus helps us understand how to bridge our divides. Jesus, who is completely holy and perfect, left the comforts of heaven to come and dwell with sinful people. He is the eternal Word made flesh. In Jesus, we see that God was not content to leave us in our sin. Instead, He came to us to share in our sorrows. This is what it means to pursue an incarnational ministry—to be present with them in their suffering.

**READ HEBREWS 4:15**

Because Jesus became human, He understands what it's like to be human. We have a God who knows what it is to hurt and to grief. He did not isolate Himself from rejection or injury. Instead, He took on flesh to become familiar with our temptation and suffering. At least part of what it means to follow Jesus is to pursue the same kind of ministry of presence. If you don't understand your brother or sister's frustration and suffering, you won't ever be moved to action. Before you can passionately say, "Tear down that wall!" you must be able to empathize with them. You can start by having a conversation.

**Who is someone you can learn from that comes from a different background than you? What are some questions you can ask to learn about their experience?**

As you take this step, remember that everyone's experience is different. It is important that we talk to people not as representatives of their culture or ethnicity, but of their own experiences.

# Tearing Down Walls

One of our natural reactions to both "the other" and to suffering is to move away from it. Tearing down walls means being proximate to the suffering and pain of others. It means experiencing it. It also means speaking up when it happens.

**Consider where you live, where your kids go to school, where you go for recreation, and where you go to church. In what ways could you put yourself in a position to interact with diverse people?**

**Do you speak up when you see injustice against people of color?**

**If you see a clear abuse of power, do you speak up in sympathy for the victim and rebuke for the aggressor? If not, why not?**

This is a difficult and complicated subject that we will study more in the coming weeks. Finish today by asking God to make you a person that seeks to sympathize and take action.

> *Pray and ask the Lord to search your heart and reveal to you hidden areas of apathy and indifference.*

Promoting Unity
Where We Live,
Work, and Worship

THE CHURCH
*and the*
RACIAL DIVIDE

**THINK**
How can you demonstrate
God's love to your neighbor?

WEEK 4

*Finding Unity in the Race-Transcending Gospel*

VOLUME IV

# Pursuing Gospel Relationships

"Love your neighbor as yourself"
— Mark 12:30

| *Renewed Thinking* | *Gospel Application* | *Faith in Action* |
| --- | --- | --- |

The gospel runs through relationships.

*Who Is My Neighbor?*

**LUKE 10:25–37**

**Loving the "others"**

John 15:12–13

Act.

THE TIME IS NOW.

*Review*

Welcome to Session 4. Use these questions to open the group session.

During last week's sessions, you read about breaking down racial barriers.

**What ideas did you find yourself most agreeing with? What ideas did you find yourself most resistant to? Why?**

**Now that we are at the mid-point of the study, what are some biblical truths you hadn't noticed before?**

*Start*

**Think about your closest friends. How did those friendships begin? What united you?**

**When has the gospel led you to pursue a conversation that seemed uncomfortable? Why is pushing through uncomfortable feelings necessary?**

Last week, we thought about breaking down barriers. This week, we will talk about establishing relationships. Most of our friendships are based on common interest or proximity—oftentimes; our relationships are based on both. But we also realize that the gospel compels us to widen our circles, to pursue relationships beyond proximity and interest. As we are united to Christ, we will pursue love towards others, because that is what Jesus has done for us.

**BEFORE WATCHING THE VIDEO, SPEND A FEW MINUTES IN PRAYER.**

*Thank God for beginning a relationship with you. Pray that your relationship with God would compel you to form relationships with others.*

Video sessions available at LifeWay.com/thechurchandtheracialdivide or with a subscription to SmallGroup.com

Dr. Sánchez opened the video by telling us how humanity's purpose is to image God by the way we rule creation. God designed people to be a display of His glory in the world, and all people failed, except one—Jesus. As followers of Jesus, our goal in life is to become increasingly like Jesus—the true image of God. If we are following Jesus, the love of Jesus will flow through us and to our neighbor.

### READ MATTHEW 22:37–40

**How is loving our neighbor connected to loving God?**

### READ ROMANS 13:8–10

**Why do you think Paul summarizes the law only as "love your neighbor as yourself?"**

**How did Jesus treat His neighbors, including neighbors who were very different than Him? How would Jesus love your neighbors differently than you?**

Though Jesus came from a Jewish family, He did not let His ethnicity keep Him from people His Jewish brothers and sisters would have cautioned Him to avoid. Jesus ate with sinners. He went out of His way to speak to a Samaritan woman (John 4). He related to her with empathy and understanding. Jesus healed people outside of the nation of Israel. He touched the untouchable. He frequently called those who oppressed and disregarded those who were vulnerable or thought to be outside of God's promises. Jesus loved His neighbors across differences. He spoke truth in love and showed us what it means to truly love our neighbors.

### READ EPHESIANS 4:15–16

**What does it mean to speak the truth in love?**

**What does it look like to also accept the truth from our brothers and sisters in love?**

**How does speaking and accepting truth in love promote unity in a diverse church?**

## *Engage*

**DR. SÁNCHEZ GIVES SEVERAL EXAMPLES OF WAYS TO
PRACTICE LOVING NEIGHBORS ACROSS ETHNIC DIVIDES.**

- Reading Scripture together that shows God's heart for the nations and our responsibility to cross barriers with the gospel.
- Watching movies with our kids that show racism as an issue and then talking about it.
- Serving the poor together to overcome socioeconomic boundaries with actual neighborly love.
- Shopping in international grocery stores to experience other cultures where you live.
- Talk with other parents and families whose paths you cross at your kids' sporting events.
- Find people different from you and have them over for dinner. Take time to listen to their story.
- Use hospitality to start relationships in your neighborhood so you can understand needs and meet them tangibly.

**Which of these ideas will you pursue over the next week?**

**Why is reading the Scriptures together essential for a family seeking
to engage different ethnicities in friendship for the sake of the gospel?**

**Who are some people you can make plans to
spend time with over the next month?**

**Where is a place you can visit as a family?**

**Brainstorm additional ways to connect and form relationships.**

---

*Ask God to forgive you when you have failed to love your neighbor
as yourself. Pray that you would show the world His heart
through the relationships you cultivate in your community.*

---

# Ideas vs. Reality

*"Love in action is a harsh and dreadful thing compared with love in dreams."*
— **FATHER ZOSSIMA, THE BROTHERS KARAMAZOV**

*"Scripture never tells us to love 'humanity' or to love 'ideals,' only to love our neighbors, all of them, one by one. 'Humanity' is a dream, neighbor is a fact.*
— **PETER KREEFT, CHRISTIANITY FOR MODERN PAGANS**

The two quotes above represent one of the hardest yet most beautiful truths of the Christian faith. God does not love ideas. He loves people. Jesus didn't say, "I have come to teach you the truth," He said, "I am the truth" (John 14:6).

God is not a theological concept. He is a person and He loves real people. Likewise, we aren't commanded to love conceptions of people. We are commanded to love real, individual, sinful, messed up, people. It's one thing to talk about the idea of loving people of other races and cultures. It's another thing entirely to love Marquez or Markeisha. Samuel or Samantha. Juan or Juanita. Chen or Cheyenne. Amari or Amanda.

Every person is different. We don't encounter people in a vacuum. We encounter people in a broken, sinful world. As much as each one of us are image-bearers of God, we are also sinners and sinned against. We have hurt people and been hurt by people. And those sins and scars make up how we see others and how we think about ourselves.

I remember when my wife and I adopted our middle son. For nearly a year before he came home, my four-year-old son Micah would spend time talking to his brother's picture. He had conversations with him, in which he would provide the responses. He would speak for his brother. Of course, the answers were always ideal.

"Isaac, would you like to play?"

"Yes, I would, Micah."

Micah met us at the airport when we got off the plane with Isaac. We buckled Isaac in, and the screaming began. Micah sat—eyes wide— not even sure what to say. His ideal was wrecked by the reality of his brother. This was not going according to plan. But we don't love pictures of our brothers; we love our brothers. We don't love ideas.

Brothers, Micah and Isaac

We love our neighbors. Let's watch God's ideal for an "all nations" gospel become real people today in Scripture.

# Peter and Cornelius

Last week you looked at the church in Antioch in Acts 11. Before those changes could happen broadly in the early church, God worked in a few individuals. Namely, Peter and Cornelius. Let's look at what's happening here.

**READ ACTS 10:1-48**

**What made it so difficult for Peter to take the gospel to Cornelius?**

Peter was hungry and dreamt of animals coming down in a sheet, then he heard a voice telling him to eat. He was baffled, because for 1400 years, the Jews had avoided eating these animals, because they were obeying God's law. God told them they were unclean.

Now, God was telling Peter to have some bacon and alligator tail. Of course, Peter protested, and he heard Jesus say, "What God has made clean, don't call common" (Acts 10:15). The prohibition on eating these animals for the Jews was a reminder of sin. It was a reminder that God had made a promise to somehow cleanse them of sin—to forgive them—and those laws and promises were unique to Israel.

Now, through this dream and through Cornelius (who is a Gentile), God was making an announcement through Peter that Jesus Christ is the way He's forgiven sin and that forgiveness was now available to everyone. In other words, this dream indicated to Peter that it was not only the Jews that could have their sins forgiven and know and worship God. In light of Christ, people from every ethnicity could worship and serve the God of Israel.

**What was the substance of Peter's message starting in verse 34?**

**How did the Gentiles respond to the message?**

**READ ACTS 11:15.**

**What connection did Peter make between the events in Acts 10 and at Pentecost (see Acts 2)?**

When the Gentiles heard the gospel, they believed it, and the Spirit of God came to them. Peter recounted these events to the Jewish leaders, acknowledging the incredible connection between Peter and the disciples.

What was happening here was reverse Pentecost. In Acts 2, tongues were given to Jewish Christians. In Acts 10, God demonstrated the Holy Spirit had come to the Gentiles by the same sign. This was not an unintelligible utterance—this was an actual language that the Jews understood. We know that because when they heard it, they knew that they were praising God. All of this only happened after Peter had his dream, and Cornelius' men came to get him.

**Why do you think God did it in that order? Why the awkward encounter of Peter and Cornelius before He sent the Holy Spirit?**

It seems like it would have been easier to have the Holy Spirit descend on the Gentiles, and then Peter could have understood his dream immediately. He could have, without hesitation, embraced the Gentiles. Or at least the idea of the Gentiles. But God spreads the gospel through relationships. He quietly sent a perplexing dream to Peter three times. He sent Cornelius' men on a hunt for Peter. And then he brought the perplexing idea colliding with an awkward ethnic encounter.

**LOOK BACK AT ACTS 10:40–41.**

Peter said that God allowed a few people to witness the resurrection of Jesus so that those few would bear the responsibility to tell others to be witnesses. And notice that the way they interacted with Jesus was relational. They "ate and drank with him after he rose from the dead" (Acts 10:41).

**Why was it important for the gospel to be transmitted through personal relationships?**

**READ ACTS 10:28.**

Peter only understood his dream when he came face-to-face with people he had previously considered unclean. The idea that God was teaching him did not become clear until Cornelius and all his Gentile friends were standing in front of Peter, ready to hear from him.

Here's the takeaway for our purposes today: The gospel runs through relationships. And the gospel pushes us across ethnic and social barriers to be witnesses to the resurrection of Jesus (v. 41) and to learn more about God and ourselves in the process (v. 28).

# Overcoming Differences

**LET'S END TODAY WITH A SELF-ASSESSMENT.**

**Peter learned something about God by stepping outside of his comfort zone. When was the last time you stepped outside your comfort zone to make a friend or serve someone?**

**What have you learned about God and yourself from spending time with people who are different than you?**

**What might it look like to share the gospel with someone when there are cultural differences?**

> *End today by asking God to create a desire in you to pursue diverse friendships.*

*Gospel Application*

# Who Is My Neighbor?

**READ LUKE 10:25–37**

If you've spent time in church, or even if you haven't, you're likely familiar with the story of the good Samaritan. However, sometimes, stories can become so familiar to us that we miss the bigger point they're making. Let's stop, ask some questions, and see what we can learn from this story.

**Why did Jesus tell this story? Who did He tell it to?**

**Who are the characters? What are they meant to teach us?**

**How would you summarize the main point of this story?**

Like much of Jesus' teaching, the good Samaritan was an answer to a question from an expert in the law. He wanted to know what Jesus thought about the law. But notice the next question in v. 29, and the motive behind it. The expert in the law asked, "Who is my neighbor?"

The question wasn't out of concern. The expert wanted to justify himself (v. 29) and define who is neighbor was. Surely his neighbors were the people who looked and thought like Him. Jesus' answer was a swift rebuke to that kind of thinking.

Jesus told a simple story about a traveler who was robbed, beaten, and left for dead on the Jericho road. The injured traveler—who Jesus described only as "a man" (v. 30), though the Jewish audience would have likely thought of the man as a Jew— was passed by both a priest and a Levite, and ultimately cared for by a Samaritan. This plot twist would have been shocking for the expert questioning Jesus.

The Samaritan represented the expert's worst enemy—the vilest person he could think of. The Samaritan who had not only the compassion to help the man in the ditch, he also had the resources. He possessed the bandages, medication, the expertise, a donkey, and the money to pay for the man's recovery in the inn.

Certainly, the priest and the Levite had the same resources, but they lacked compassion. Justice, righteousness, and neighborly love were mere concepts to them. But to this Samaritan, who was thought to be doctrinally and racially impure, love was an action. Love was embodied.

The expert in the law wasn't only surprised that a Samaritan was also his neighbor, he was surprised that the Samaritan was the one giving the help Jesus called for, instead of the one receiving it.

This parable looks into our hearts and challenges our assumptions about who we believe our neighbor to be. We are all more like the expert in the law than we would ever care to admit. We are all tempted to see ourselves as above need and as the ones with all the answers. Jesus shows us that's not the case.

**Have you ever considered that you might be the one who needs someone to help you?**

**When you think about other ethnicities, do you see yourself as a Samaritan (a person who can give help) or as the person in the ditch (a person who needs to be helped)?**

**How does that attitude impact the way you think about others?**

**How can your church's short term mission trips or local missions reach and help those outside of your ethnicity with compassion and appreciation for the people you are serving?**

As the dominant culture in America, many people can perceive themselves in the role of "the hero." When this happens, they miss the opportunity to learn from the perspective of ethnic minorities. Seeing yourself as a hero keeps you from fully appreciating the contributions of others who are different than you. It also takes the idea of inconvenient love and makes it a matter of pride. From mission trips to other countries, to volunteering in an "urban ministry," the members of the dominant culture can quickly forget that they need the neighborly ministry of the minority, too.

Neighborly love doesn't just flow from dominant to weak, and rich to poor. The good Samaritan shows us that help often comes from unexpected sources. Love shows up in surprising ways for people whose strength comes out of our weakness.

**How does the gospel undo our superficial understanding of the way we relate to other people who are different than us?**

**How has today's study challenged the way you think about serving others?**

*End your time by asking God to help you become a better neighbor. Pray that the Spirit would challenge your assumptions and motivations and help you to see your neighbors through the lens of the gospel before and beyond any other identifying factor.*

# Greater Love

### READ JOHN 15:12–13

Jesus commanded us to love others as He loved us, specifically, through dying to our own preferences and lifting others up above ourselves. For the last two days, you've worked through the idea that "loving our neighbor" cannot merely remain a concept that stays on a coffee cup or t-shirt. It must be embodied and lived out in relationships. Today, as we work to put our faith into action, and to obey Jesus' commands to lay our lives down for others in love, let's brainstorm some ideas.

**Stop and pray right now for God to bring to mind some names or faces of people (friends, strangers, or enemies) to whom He is calling you to show sacrificial love.**

**On the opposite page, write those names down, along with a loving action you plan to take toward each person. Then put it on your calendar. Write down a date that you plan to take this step of love.**

*Finish today by meditating on 2 Timothy 1:7 and then asking the Lord to empower you with love and boldness to follow through with these steps of embodied neighborly love.*

# Loving My Neighbor

| Name | Loving Action | Date |
|------|---------------|------|
| | | |
| | | |
| | | |
| | | |
| | | |
| | | |
| | | |
| | | |
| | | |
| | | |
| | | |
| | | |
| | | |
| | | |
| | | |
| | | |
| | | |
| | | |
| | | |
| | | |

Act justly, love mercy,
walk humbly.
MICAH 6:8

THE CHURCH
*and the*
RACIAL DIVIDE

THINK
How are you pursuing
justice in your community?

WEEK 5 | *Finding Unity in the Race-Transcending Gospel* | VOLUME V

# Race and Culture

I have a dream that one day every valley shall be exalted, every hill and mountain shall be made low, the rough places will be made plain, and the crooked places will be made straight, and the glory of the Lord shall be revealed, and all flesh shall see it together.

MARTIN LUTHER KING, JR.

| *Renewed Thinking* | *Gospel Application* | *Faith in Action* |
| --- | --- | --- |

**AMOS 5:24**
But let justice flow like water,
and righteousness,
like an unfailing stream.

**Visions of
Restoration**

MATTHEW 23:23

## More Than
## Personal
## Holiness

*Listen*

**James 1:19–26**

## *Review*

During last week's sessions, you read about putting love into action in real relationships.

**Can anyone share ways when you or someone you
know practiced "inconvenient love?"**

**Did God bring to mind any names of people that He is calling you
to love tangibly? If so, would you share a little bit of that calling?**

## *Start*

We might all agree that the world's biggest problem is sin. But many people think differently about the specifics of how sin causes problems in the world. As an experiment in this group, let's take a poll:

**How many of you think that the world's biggest problem is individual
sin—people's deliberate choices to disregard God and act selfishly?**

**How many of you think that the world's biggest problem is sinful
and broken systems—governments, communities, and businesses
that are operating in a way that takes advantage of them?**

Today, we're going to see that the Bible addresses both of these individual and communal sins. The Bible sees sin as both personal and communal. In other words, sin isn't an "either/or" issue, but a "both/and" issue. This week we're going to talk about race and justice. This is a loaded issue that has the potential for disagreement. So let's pray for God to give us a spirit of unity and understanding.

*Discuss*

**READ JAMES 2:1–4; 3:6; 5:3–4**

**How do these verses show that injustice is both personal and societal?**

Dr. Moore defined justice as the standard that God expects in our personal lives, our corporate lives together as the church, and in communities and social and political institutions. Personal sin always translates into societal sin because society is comprised of sinful people. We should not overemphasize one to the neglect of the other.

**Dr. Moore mentioned various studies that demonstrate majority groups and minority groups view injustice differently. Why do we tend to prefer to think of sin and justice in only one of these categories?**

**What are a few simple steps we could take to better listen to one another and find areas of agreement?**

**What might a person be overlooking when they evaluate the presence of racial injustice only on the basis of personal sin (not hearing racial slurs or having personal animosity toward other races)?**

**What are some examples of systemic injustices that you might be overlooking if you only focus on personal sin?**

**How is the church called to address both personal sin and systemic injustice?**

Dr. Moore boils the church's pursuit of justice down to the following:

1. Teaching about justice
2. Embodying that teaching

**READ ACTS 6:1–7**

The early church ministered holistically by teaching about Jesus and then living out that teaching in their daily ministry.

How does this passage show the early church prioritizing
*both* the teaching of the Word *and* the embodiment
of that teaching in an act of racial justice?

What is the result of their practice (see v 7–9)?
What can we learn from their example?

## Engage

Dr. Moore finished with the following questions for us to talk about and consider:

What issues of injustice are present in your community
that you've never thought of before?

Are all people welcome in our church? Do we embody unity?
Who might feel ostracized or unwelcome among us?

What are the major tensions and the division
points in culture regarding racial injustice? How
is our church helping ease these tensions?

If we aren't pressing into these tensions, where could we start?

---

*Ask God to do work in the lives of each person as they engage the
individual sessions of the Bible study this week. Particularly, ask
God to give each person both a strong sense of personal sin and
repentance and systemic sin and repentance as it concerns racism.*

# A Prophetic Voice

Martin Luther King, Jr. delivered many speeches and wrote a great number of letters, many of which have been kept for posterity. But there is one speech and one letter in particular that most people remember.

In April of 1963, King was arrested during a nonviolent protest in Birmingham, Alabama. While in jail, he read a newspaper article authored by several white pastors from Birmingham who agreed that injustice toward blacks existed, but the proper place to fight this battle was in the courtroom, not in the streets. Additionally, they said that King was an "outsider" that had no business causing trouble in their city.

King responded with the now-famous Letter from Birmingham Jail:

"I am in Birmingham because injustice is here. Just as the eighth-century [BC] prophets left their little villages and carried their 'thus saith the Lord' far beyond the boundaries of their hometowns... I too, am compelled to carry the gospel of freedom beyond my particular hometown."

The rest of that letter implores the white "moderates" of Birmingham to take action; to join in the nonviolent demonstration against the injustices of segregation because "injustice anywhere is a threat to justice everywhere." Four months after that letter, Dr. King gave his most remembered speech from the steps of the Lincoln Memorial. Many of King's words reflected ancient truth from the biblical prophets.

"We will not be satisfied until justice rolls down like waters and righteousness like a mighty stream."

"I have a dream that one day every valley shall be exalted, every hill and mountain shall be made low, the rough places will be made plain, and the crooked places will be made straight, and the glory of the Lord shall be revealed, and all flesh shall see it together."

Dr. King not only quoted Old Testament prophets but patterned his action and response to injustice from biblical prophets. Particularly in these documents, King quoted the prophets, Isaiah and Amos.

Today, we're going to look at the biblical idea of justice, especially through the lens of biblical prophecy.

Martin Luther King, Jr, sitting in the Jefferson County Jail, in Birmingham, Alabama, 11/3/67. Everett/CSU Archives.

**BEFORE LOOKING INTO THE SCRIPTURES
CONSIDER THE FOLLOWING QUESTIONS**

What is justice? How would you define it?

Is it possible to care about societal justice and personal
sin at the same time? Why or why not?

Do you believe justice is at odds with the gospel? Explain.

The prophet Amos saw a deep connection between our worship of God and our concern (or lack thereof) for justice. He was a shepherd and a farmer in Judah, not an elected official or an appointed king. He easily could have minded his own business and just tended his flock and protected his fig trees. But God called him to something more, namely, to confront the northern kingdom of Israel under Jeroboam's rule. Jeroboam had allowed idolatry and injustices to go on in Israel because they were making the country wealthy. Israel's sin was both spiritual and social in nature. They were guilty of both idolatry and injustice.

# Hear This Word

**READ AMOS 2:6; 4:1; 5:11–12**

What injustice did Amos mention in these verses?
What might be examples of these today?

These verses outline some of the injustices happening in Israel. People were being sold for money and traded for material goods (2:1). Those in positions of power were oppressing the poor, and they were callous to their sin, choosing instead to indulge in alcohol (4:1).

They were overtaxing the poor for basic food needs, while they pursued lavish lifestyles of elegant houses and vineyards. The wealthy and powerful in Israel were using their wealth and power to gain more wealth and keep their power at the expense of the weak and poor (5:11–12).

# Justice and Righteousness

### READ AMOS 5:4–7,14–15, 21–24

**How are right worship and the pursuit of justice connected in Amos?**

The Lord told Israel to stop worshiping false gods and indulging in the apathetic lifestyles of comfort that led to injustice and, instead, to seek God and seek good (5:6,14). Think about that for a minute. Seeking God and seeking justice are not separate issues. Worshiping idols and perpetuating social ills are related activities. Both demand repentance that requires real action.

The Lord told Israel that all the religious fervor and ritual they could muster were meaningless to Him if they refused to repent of the injustice they both participated in and ignored for so long. And then we get to the verse famously quoted by Martin Luther King Jr. in his speech from the Lincoln Memorial. Instead of offering empty worship that is disconnected from caring about the needs of their neighbors, Israel was commanded to "let justice flow like water and righteousness like an unfailing stream." From God's perspective, justice and righteousness are deeply connected.

**When have you disconnected what God has connected in His Word?**

Righteousness refers to people in right relationship to God and each other. It means that people live together as image-bearers of God and treat each other with dignity and respect. That despite social and economic differences, people are treated fairly and with honor. Righteousness has a lot to do with how we personally act towards one another.

Justice refers to taking action to bring back right relationships and restore fairness and dignity in the systems that humans live in. Justice has a lot to do with our community and governments.

Through the prophet Amos, God is telling His people, "Live in right relationship with God and with all people. When you find human beings whose dignity is being trampled on, you should take action to restore them to right relationship with their God and their fellow man."

**How does what Amos is saying compare with
what Jesus said in Matthew 22:37–39?**

# Restoration

### READ AMOS 9:11–15

At the end of the book, Amos gives us a picture of the kingdom of God. Surprisingly, it's filled with a lot of the things that God took from Israel during His judgment. Rather than scarcity, there is abundance for everyone. There is a river, not of justice and righteousness, but of joy—the fruit of justice and righteousness. Wine is a celebratory drink. It represents joy. Amos envisioned a look ahead to the New Jerusalem, where righteousness and justice are perfect (Rev. 21:1–2).

When Martin Luther King, Jr. gave his vision for an America where righteousness and justice flowed like a mighty river, he borrowed from this biblical vision of the new heavens and new earth. In a way, he was praying as Jesus taught us to pray, "Your will be done, on earth, as it is in heaven" (Matt. 5:10).

Prophets don't just deliver judgment for injustice in Scripture; they also give a vision for a future. Jesus preached about the coming kingdom of God. It was an indictment of the evil practices of Pharisees, and hope for tax collectors and sinners. It was a vision of the world remade—one like Dr. King delivered from the Lincoln memorial.

**TAKE A MOMENT TO REFLECT ON JUSTICE, RIGHTEOUSNESS, AND THE WARNINGS OF AMOS.**

**What needs to change in your own thinking based on God's Word?**

**How have you chosen convenience and comfort over the good of your neighbor?**

**Having worked through this personal study, how would you say we are called to pursue justice?**

**How are you personally seeking the good of others by obeying God's commands to pursue justice?**

*Gospel Application*

# God of Love. God of Justice.

The gospel teaches us that all have fallen short of God's standard of righteousness. Because of our sin, we are condemned and separated from our Father. And yet, despite our sin, God Himself has paid the price for our disobedience on the cross. Because of Jesus, we will be with God for all of eternity.

However, the Bible is filled with commands about personal holiness and righteousness. Why? Not because God is asking us to pay Him back for His grace, but because the goal of our salvation is that we, as individuals become like Jesus (Rom. 8:29). Unfortunately, that is where many Christians stop thinking about the implications of the gospel—at our personal righteousness. In doing so, we miss how our personal salvation is meant to impact the world around us.

### READ MATTHEW 23:23

### How would you summarize what Jesus is saying here?

As Jesus pronounced a series of "woes" to the Pharisees, He pointed out that the Pharisees have an otherwise commendable righteousness, extending to the smallest of details. They were so committed to the personal discipline of giving ten percent, that they were even giving that sum of their spices to the Lord. Yet in spite of this, Jesus said, "you neglect justice, mercy, and faithfulness." In other words, you pay attention to these small personal matters, but you are completely ignoring injustice happening to your neighbors.

In the gospels, Jesus' swiftest rebukes were given to the ruling religious elite. He found a people who were so concerned with their own personal piety and righteousness that they had ignored caring for their neighbors.

### What injustices might you be tempted to ignore
### as you practice personal righteousness?

### Why do we pay attention to personal implications of the gospel (like receiving forgiveness or living holy lives), but ignore communal implications of the gospel?

The temptation to pay attention only to individual and personal matters, but ignore larger systemic matters of justice is well illustrated in the following parable.

*There was a small town built next to a large river. Unexpectedly one day, some of the townsfolk saw a child's body floating down the river. A woman rushed into the river, brought the child to shore, resuscitated the child and then cared for her. The next day, more children floated down the river. Some were dead, and so the town arranged funerals for them. Others were still alive. They were each rescued and the townsfolk ensured they were properly cared for and integrated into the life of the town. As it became evident that each day that there would be more and more babies to rescue, the townsfolk developed a rescue system —from those that would pull them out of the river all the way to those responsible for enrolling them in school and finding them a home. Each year, the town held a gala to honor those who served the children. Awards were given for the courage, bravery, and rescue innovation. Many years later, after that very first rescued child had grown up, she was invited to the gala to present an award and offer thanks for the efforts of the town. By this time, the town took much pride in their child-rescue efforts. When the young lady stepped upon the stage to address the crowd she said, "I'm grateful for the woman who rescued me. And I'm grateful to see the love and attention of all the people involved in the rescue of the children that have helplessly followed me down that river for the last 20 years. However, I have one question that I would humbly ask. Has anyone yet been upstream to see why these children keep turning up in this river?"*

In the parable, the issue is not that the townspeople don't care about the children floating down the river. They encounter each child individually with love and care. The issue is that they refuse to think about why people are dying upstream. That's a justice issue. That's what the Pharisees were neglecting. Jesus wasn't condemning their acts of personal piety—He was condemning their willful ignorance of justice.

**READ PROVERBS 31:8–9 AND DEUTERONOMY 10:17–22.**

**How does God relate His character to His justice?**

**Why do you think God addresses justice in
the Scripture as often as He does?**

Up to this point in this study, we've established that God cares about all ethnicities living in peace with Him and each other. Today, we've seen that He cares deeply about justice. These issues are repeatedly addressed in God's Word because they are both close to His heart. If we are God's people, we must reflect God's heart.

**So, if a lack of compassion for and attention to issues of justice is one of
the major barriers to ethnic harmony in our culture, what steps will you
take to reflect God's heart by beginning pursuing justice around you?**

# Understanding Systemic Injustice

Most people have no problem acknowledging the existence of personal sin. Fewer people recognize the presence of systemic, societal injustice. For some of us working through this study, seeing systemic injustice might be difficult because we have not experienced it. Today we're going to take a closer look at systemic injustice.

To understand how Christ might call the church to respond, we need to examine the broader storyline of racial injustice to see its root and fruit. Today, let's take a look at the need for justice as it concerns race in our country in the 21st century.

**What are some areas of society where you see both personal and systemic sin? For instance, would you consider legal abortion a system that aligns against the vulnerable?**

**Why is it important for Christians to think through both personal and corporate dimensions to the Fall?**

In the 17th–18th century, Africans were abducted from their home country and shipped across the Atlantic, enduring horrifically inhumane conditions. These men, women, and children were forced to be slaves—a source of cheap labor for the economic development of early America. This economic system primarily benefited white people as black people were treated as property.

In an effort to protect the financial prosperity befalling America through slavery, several false storylines were developed regarding race. Pseudoscientific theories were developed about the sizes of skulls for different races and what that indicated about intelligence. Faulty theological theories that black people were descendants of Ham (Gen. 9) and were cursed into slavery began to spread. Race and ethnicity were not seen as an indicator of unique ways God could display His glory in people, but rather, race became an indicator of what sort of life a person was allowed to live.

By 1865, the law emancipated all slaves. But that one act could not automatically correcy centuries of injustice. Believing that racial strife ended with slavery misses the reality that an entire economic and social system that is based on slavery can't change overnight. Additionally, the emancipated slaves did not suddenly have the financial resources or social clout to open up a store in the town square to be financially self-sufficient.

The inequality rooted in the injustice of slavery continued for decades through Jim Crow laws, and other legal statutes implicitly or explicitly designed to deny the rights of millions. While slavery and Jim Crow laws have been outlawed, the lingering effects of systemic racism still remain in our country.

Systemic injustice is complicated and nuanced. Obviously, a few pages in a Bible study isn't enough space to give serious thought to the whole history of racial injustice, but it's a starting point. The goal of this study is to begin a conversation around these issues and give you practical handles for how to engage them beyond this study.

# Listen

—

Understanding injustice isn't something that can happen in a day, but you can start walking step by step toward understanding. Below are some starting points. But before you begin, meditate on these words from James.

*Know this, my beloved brothers: let every person be quick to hear, slow to speak,*
*slow to anger; for the anger of man does not produce the righteousness of God.*
**JAMES 1:19–20**

**Several places in this study have encouraged you to begin a dialog**
**with someone from a different ethnicity. Have you taken this**
**step? If so, what did you learn? Reflect in the space below.**

**If you haven't taken this step, why haven't you?**
**What is keeping you from reaching out?**

As you develop relationships across ethnic lines, take the time to ask new friends to share their experience. You may not agree with everything that is said, but your goal is not to agree but to listen to their experience. Once again, remember that all people are individuals, and their experiences may differ from others with whom they share a cultural heritage.

**How could you be a better friend and listener**
**to people who are different than you?**

**Think about the last time you heard someone express their experience**
**with systemic injustice. Did you listen? Or did you tune them out**
**because their experience didn't square with your opinion?**

**What would it look like to put James 1:19–20 into**
**practice in your conversations on race?**

# Where Do We Go from Here?

"The true measure of our character is how we treat the poor, the disfavored, the accused, the incarcerated, and the condemned."

**BRYAN STEVENSON**

| *Renewed Thinking* | *Gospel Application* | *Faith In Action* |
| --- | --- | --- |
| **FREEDOM FOR DEATH ROW INMATE** | *Seek Things Above* | Don't Grow Weary In Doing Good |
| *Matthew 25:31-46* | COLOSSIANS 3:1-3 | GALATIANS 6:9 |

## *Review*

> **Welcome to our final session. Use these questions to open the group session.**

Last week's sessions may have presented some unique challenges to you, as we dove into ideas about systemic racial injustice.

**Will someone share about any difficulties you had understanding or believing the material you encountered this week?**

**Has God begun to shift your thinking regarding systemic racism in any way? Why or why not?**

## *Start*

**What is a big problem you've solved by taking small steps?**

Have you ever heard the parable of the starfish?

It goes like this.

Once a man was walking on a beach where the tide had washed up hundreds and hundreds of starfish. Some of them were already dead, but many others were still alive, being threatened by the hot sun as the water pushed them further and further up on the sand. Then, the man noticed a little boy frantically picking up one starfish at a time and flinging it, as far as he could, back into the ocean. The man asked the boy, "What are you doing?"

The boy replied, "I'm saving these starfish."

"But there are so many. You can't possibly make a difference to all these starfish."

The boy hurled another one out into the deep, then turned and looked at the man. "I made a difference to that one."

There is a reason that parable sounds cliché. Like many clichés—it illustrates a deep and resounding truth. When faced with an insurmountable problem, we should start small. This week we are going to focus on incremental steps we can take to pursue reconciliation across the racial divide.

Video sessions available at LifeWay.com/thechurchandtheracialdivide or with a subscription to SmallGroup.com

Discuss

In the video, Trevor noted that we need to have an ongoing vision of the future kingdom of God to shape how we live in the present. Let's take a look at a picture of the future kingdom of God.

READ REVELATION 22:1–3

In the new heavens and new earth that Jesus is bringing, John gives us a picture of a city street with a river, a tree of life filled with fruit, and the leaves of a tree that are used to heal the nations.

> **Remembering that "nations" means "ethnicities," what do you think the healing of nations might look like in heaven?**

> **How would people of different ethnicities act toward one another in this city of God?**

> **What does it mean that "there will no longer be any curse?"**

The first step in acting on our convictions of racial reconciliation is to keep in our minds the vision of "all nations healed, worshiping Christ, without any curse."

> **As followers of Jesus, we are called to bring the kingdom of heaven to bear on the world around us. How should knowing that we will all one day be reconciled to one another change how we live today?**

> **What are some ways we can keep one another focused on this vision of the kingdom of God?**

Trevor used Nehemiah as a template for our response to racial injustice and how we should take action. You'll study this more in-depth this week in your individual Bible study.

READ NEHEMIAH 1:3–4

> **What was Nehemiah's response to the trouble in Jerusalem?**

> **How should our response to injustice be like Nehemiah's?**

**READ NEHEMIAH 1:6–7**

Nehemiah starts his prayer with confession of sin and repentance. He confessed his own sin and genuinely acknowledged the failing of Israel that led to the exile. It is not enough to recognize our own sin; we need to offer recognition and heartfelt lament for historic injustice.

**Though people living today are not directly responsible
for slavery, why is it important to acknowledge and lament
this and other historical injustices against minorities?**

**What message does it send to our minority brothers
and sisters when we are dismissive of them and do not
acknowledge or empathize with their hurt?**

*Engage*

Let's end this the group portion of this Bible study talking about where we go from here. What action can we take together and as individuals?

**What are some ways you have been challenged by this study.**

**What actions will you take as a result of this study?**

Let's end this group time in a confessional and faith-filled prayer. Leave the next several minutes open to spontaneous prayers confessing sin, repenting, and asking God for faith to take action toward unity and love across ethnic boundaries.

*Close the time in prayer with a prayer for your group to keep this
conversation going in their families, their church, and their communities.*

# Concern for the Least

Walter McMillian, a black man, was convicted and sentenced to death for the murder of a young white woman in Monroeville, Alabama, in the 1980s.

His trial lasted less than two days. Though multiple witnesses corroborated McMillian's alibi, he was at a fish fry at the time of the murder, all those witnesses were black. The jury gave him life in prison. The judge decided that wasn't enough. Walter McMillian was sentenced to death.

Bryan Stevenson was a young law student when he met his first prisoner on death row in 1983. It changed his life. From that moment, Bryan committed his life to helping the poor and unjustly imprisoned. In 1993, six years after Walter McMillian was condemned to die for a crime he didn't commit, Bryan Stevenson proved that he was a victim of racist lies, and McMillian was released.

Following that victory, Stevenson started the Equal Justice Initiative (EJI). Since its inception, "EJI has won major legal challenges eliminating excessive and unfair sentencing, exonerating innocent death row prisoners, confronting abuse of the incarcerated and the mentally ill, and aiding children prosecuted as adults." Mr. Stevenson and his staff have won reversals, relief, or release from prison for over 135 wrongly condemned prisoners on death row and won relief for hundreds of others wrongly convicted or unfairly sentenced.

Mr. Stevenson has argued and won multiple cases at the United States Supreme Court, including a 2019 ruling protecting condemned prisoners who suffer from dementia and a landmark 2012 ruling that banned mandatory life-imprison-ment-without-parole sentences for all children seventeen years old or younger. Mr. Stevenson has initiated major new anti-poverty and anti-discrimination efforts that challenge inequality in America. He led the creation of two highly acclaimed cultural sites which opened in 2018: the Legacy Museum and the National Memorial for Peace and Justice

These new national landmark institutions chronicle the legacy of slavery, lynching, and racial segregation, and the connection to mass incarceration and con-temporary issues of racial bias."[1] Stevenson said, "I've come to believe that the true measure of our commitment to justice, the character of our society, our commitment to the rule of law, fairness, and equality cannot be measured by how we treat the

Walter McMilllan (from left), his granddaughter, his wife Minnie McMillian, attorney and author Bryan Stevenson and Walter's sister Eva lene Smith gather outside the court house after Walter's release from prison. McMilllan spent six years on death row for a murder he did not commit. Photo: Equal Justice Initiative

rich, the powerful, the privileged, and the respected among us. The true measure of our character is how we treat the poor, the disfavored, the accused, the incarcerated, and the condemned."[2] The Scriptures teach us that Jesus will hold us accountable for how we treat the least among us.

### READ MATTHEW 25:31–46

**How does this teaching from Jesus help us understand what it looks like to advocate for the marginalized and oppressed?**

1. EJI.org website https://eji.org/bryan-stevenson
2. Bryan Stevenson, *Just Mercy*. 18.

Though our righteousness is secure in Jesus, there will come a day when we stand before Jesus and account for how we have lived. On that day, Jesus will question us about how we treated the poor, the marginalized, the powerless, and the vulnerable.

This is an overwhelming truth. You are probably asking, "How do I help? What should I do? Now that I know this injustice exists—where do I go from here?"

Taking a step may seem overwhelming, but all we need to do is take one step. We can take heart in Jesus' words, who told us that the kingdom of God is made up of small steps of faith, and showed us that even helping one person in need of justice makes an eternal difference.

# Learning from Nehemiah

Nehemiah was someone who was living in luxury and then got news of a marginalized people who were unjustly suffering. Let's see what the Lord can teach us through his example.

### READ NEHEMIAH 1–2

Nehemiah is the king's cupbearer (1:11). This means that he was in a position of authority and privilege with access to resources that the people of Jerusalem didn't have. Day after day, he sat next to the king. Meanwhile, Jerusalem was in ruins following a relatively unsuccessful attempt to rebuild it after the Babylonian exile. They were continually being threatened and taken advantage of.

**How did Nehemiah use his position in the king's court, to help the people of Jerusalem?**

**Before Nehemiah put an action plan into motion, what things did he do? (See 1:4, 1:6, & 2:4)**

Nehemiah's response to the report of the "great trouble and shame" in Jerusalem can teach us about our response to racial injustice in our country. Here are four sets of actions that Nehemiah took that are relevant to the question, "What do I do about racism and injustice?"

# Practical Steps

## 1. LISTEN AND LAMENT (1:4, 2:3)

- Nehemiah listened to the report and took it seriously.

- He didn't pass blame or say, "Well, you should have never moved back to Jerusalem. If you would have stayed in Babylon with me, you could have the life I have."

- He didn't ask them to prove injustice over and over.

- Instead, he listened and wept with them.

- Nehemiah lamented. and mourned their condition. He hurt with them and showed emphathy.

**Where do you need to lament over the disunity
and strife in our culture?**

**Why don't we make time in our prayer lives
to lament as Nehemiah did?**

## 2. CONFESS AND REPENT (1:6–10)

- Nehemiah confessed his sin and lamented the sins of his ancestors. He didn't say, "Well, Israel is in a mess, but I didn't have anything to do with that. It wasn't *my sin* that got us into exile." Instead, he identified with Israel and confessed sin and acknowledged the historic failings of those who came before.

   **As you've worked through this study, has God brought to mind any specific areas where you need to confess, repent, and seek reconciliation? How are you pursuing this?**

## 3. PRAY AND PRACTICE GOD'S PRESENCE (1:4,11, 2:4–5)

- Nehemiah's first response was prayer and fasting. His lament wasn't just feeling bad for people; it was directed to the Lord in the hope that He would answer.

- Nehemiah took a bold action step by asking for the king's help, but even as he spoke, he was praying.

   **Does your lament turn into action, or are you content in inaction? Who could you bless with sympathetic presence?**

## 4. BE PROXIMATE TO SUFFERING, USE YOUR POSITION, AND EXPECT OPPOSITION (2:5–20)

- On one hand, Nehemiah could have shown up in Jerusalem for a photo op, sort of like the President flying over a disaster area. On the other hand, he could have gone to the king and asked for aid to be air-dropped in by parachute while he stayed in the palace. But Nehemiah didn't take the easy way out.

- Nehemiah went to Jerusalem. He saw it with his own eyes and moved there. He let go of his status to get shoulder-to-shoulder with the suffering.

- Nehemiah used his position with the king to get resources to build the wall. He leveraged the position he had, but didn't use it to his own advantage.

- Nehemiah was willing to face opposition. Sanballat, Tobiah, and Geshem mocked and opposed him. They accused him of being a traitor. But Nehemiah continued the work, appealing to God as the one able to make things happen.

- Whenever you are doing something that brings justice and healing that threaten someone else's way of life, expect criticism and opposition.

**How can you work to alleviate suffering around you?**

**Why should you hold fast to God's good
work even when it becomes hard?**

**Of the four categories discussed, which do you have the
hardest time doing? Why do you think that is?**

# Seek the Things Above

**READ COLOSSIANS 3:1–5, GALATIANS 6:8–9, AND 2 CORINTHIANS 4:16–8**

These verses have something in common—a heavenly vision. In Colossians, Paul tells us to set our mind on heavenly things—namely, what Christ's death and resurrection accomplished.

In 2 Corinthians, Paul tells us to dwell on what the coming kingdom of God will be like, not on the state of the brokenness of the world. In other words, in the current reality of a world broken and falling apart with sin, keep a picture of the future reality of God's new heavens and new earth in your day-to-day vision.

Here's the point: Racial reconciliation and justice is difficult work. Seeing the brokenness and futility of worldly systems and hateful people can keep your focus on the temporary, while you lose sight of the beautiful future to which we are called. You'll get tired of doing good and want to give up.

Without a deep relationship with God in Christ and a firm vision of the multiethnic kingdom He desires, we will lose the will for racial reconciliation and justice and give up.

### ANSWER THE FOLLOWING QUESTIONS HONESTLY.

**Do you make it a priority to read Scripture, meditate on God's Word, and pray as a daily habit? If so, does that habit refresh you or drain you? Why?**

**Are you able to tell the difference between the days when you are immersed in Scripture versus the days that you aren't? If so, what's the difference?**

One of the goals of this study is to help you think biblically about race and culture. At least part of the reason we are so divided as a culture and a church is because we allow cultural voices to shape our thinking more than the Bible. If our desire is to seek and please Christ, we must seek Him and His wisdom more than we seek human wisdom.

Read Paul's words to the church at Colossae again.

> *So if you have been raised with Christ, seek the things above, where Christ is, seated at the right hand of God. Set your minds on things above, not on earthly things. For you died, and your life is hidden with Christ in God. When Christ, who is your life, appears, then you also will appear with him in glory. Therefore, put to death what belongs to your earthly nature*
> **COLOSSIANS 3:1–5**

### How is the call to put to death what is earthly in us related to our resurrection with Christ?

### What does it mean to "put to death what belongs to your earthly nature"? What is an example of a habit, behavior, or attitude in your life that needs to be "put to death"?

### How do these habits, behaviors, and attitudes, keep you from seeking "the things above?

Being raised with Christ means that we are Christians—we belong to Him. The gospel fundamentally changes who we are. But the gospel doesn't stop there; it also transforms the way we live. Being raised with Christ also entails putting to death what is earthly in us.

Ethnic division among the church comes from our earthly nature and must be put to death in order to seek the things that are above. Here at the end of the study we need to stop and consider how the voices we let into our lives shape us. Here's a question to get you started down that path:

**When you talk about matters of race, is the conversation informed more by your political leanings or biblical ideas regarding human dignity and God's glory? Why?**

## IN THE SPACE BELOW, TAKE AN "INFLUENCE INVENTORY" TO SEE WHAT'S SHAPING YOU.

Hours per week reading Scripture _____

Hours per week in meditating on Scripture/journaling/prayer ____

Hours per week spent on social media _____

Do the people you follow represent diverse viewpoints? Yes / No

Do the news organizations you follow represent diverse viewpoints? Yes / No

Hour per week taking in news _____

Hours per week watching TV/Movies_____

List some of your regular TV shows?

What unhelpful messages are you taking in through these shows?

Look back on Colossians 3:1–5 and compare to your
influence inventory. Do you think your views on race
are being shaped by Christ or something else?

Spend time in confession, repentance, and prayer. Ask God
to help you prioritize His vision of race & justice.

List any changes you think you need to make below.

1.

2.

3.

4.

5.

# Take a Step

The racial divide in our country is contrary to the unified multiethnic vision of the kingdom of God. The problem is complicated. There are no simple solutions. It's filled with pitfalls and dangerous temptations to get involved in political arguments, giving ourselves over to anger that doesn't lead to God's righteousness (Jas. 1:19–20). It can feel insurmountable. It's so much easier to check out of the problem.

But we are not to grow weary in doing good (Gal. 6:9). So here are four suggestions to get started (in no particular order).

### 1. GET PROXIMATE TO SUFFERING. MAKE IT "YOUR PROBLEM" INSTEAD OF SOMEONE ELSE'S.

- This is a difficult step not only to do but even to see. Start with prayer—"God, show me where people in my town/city are suffering from racism or racial injustice."

- What pattern in your life can you change to get someone across the table from you to love and hear about their experiences?

### 2. USE RELATIONSHIPS TO BRING ATTENTION TO RACIAL INJUSTICE AND THE MULTIETHNIC KINGDOM OF GOD.

- Are you a pastor? Preach about it.

- Are you a member of a church? Talk to your pastor about it.

- When you hear racist comments, speak up.

- Are you an influencer in your community? Draw attention to people who are suffering injustice but are being overlooked.

- Initiate discussions with people in your sphere of influence and help educate on issues of racial unity.

- Invite them to talk about what you've learned.

## 3. FIND WAYS TO SERVE THROUGH ORGANIZATIONS.

- What are the ministries or non-profits in your town doing work with victims of racial injustice? Find them and set up some meetings to understand the work they are doing and how you might volunteer.

## 4. PLACE YOURSELF UNDER DIVERSE LEADERSHIP.

- Often, the most simple step of humility and growth is to serve underneath someone.

- God may be calling you to join a church where you are the minority.

- He may be asking you to step aside from the group you are leading and invite a person of a different race to lead.

- Maybe this isn't even formal leadership. Perhaps you ask a faithful Christian of a different race to lead you in one-on-one discipleship.

Let's end with a vision of God's multiethnic kingdom that He will bring in full when Christ returns. In Revelation 21–22, we get the vision of the new Jerusalem, the one that Nehemiah dreamed of and worked toward, coming down out of heaven prepared by God. Keep in mind the word "nations" refers to ethnic people groups.

**Read Revelation 21:14, 22–7, 22:1–5. With that vision of
the kingdom, pray the Lord's Prayer out loud.**

# Leader Guide

## PREPARE TO LEAD

Watch the session's teaching video and read the group content with the leader guide tear-out in hand to understand how it supplements each section of the group study. Spend time praying for each group member by name asking God to use the group to transform their heart.

## CONSIDERATIONS

Race can be a difficult topic to discuss with other people. These sessions will uncover sin and for us to reckon with difficult truths. This section should help you do be aware of potential issues.

## RESOURCES

For each week of the study we have included additional resources to aid in your study and to send out to your group as you see fit.

# Tips for Leading a Small Group

**FOLLOW THESE GUIDELINES TO PREPARE FOR EACH SESSION.**

# Prayerfully Prepare

**REVIEW.** Review the personal studies and group questions ahead of time.

**PRAY.** Be intentional about praying for each person in the group. Ask the Holy Spirit to work through you and the group discussion as you point group members to Jesus each week through God's Word.

# Minimize Distractions

Create a comfortable environment. If group members are uncomfortable, they'll be distracted and, therefore, not engaged in the group experience. Plan ahead by considering these details:

Seating
Temperature
Lighting
Food or drink
Surrounding noise
General cleanliness

At best, thoughtfulness and hospitality show guests and group members they're welcome and valued in whatever environment you choose to gather. At worst, people may never notice your effort, but they're also not distracted. Do everything in your ability to help people focus on what's most important: connecting with God, with the Bible, and with one another.

# Include Others

Your goal is to foster a community in which people are welcome just as they are but encouraged to grow spiritually. Always be aware of opportunities to include any people who visit the group and to invite new people to join your group. An inexpensive way to make first-time guests feel welcome or to invite someone to get involved is to give them their own copies of this Bible-study book.

# Encourage Discussion

A good small-group experience has the following characteristics.

**EVERYONE PARTICIPATES.** Encourage everyone to ask questions, share responses, or read aloud.

**NO ONE DOMINATES—NOT EVEN THE LEADER.** Be sure that your time speaking as a leader takes up less than half of your time together as a group. Politely guide discussion if anyone dominates.

**NOBODY IS RUSHED THROUGH QUESTIONS.** Don't feel that a moment of silence is a bad thing. People often need time to think about their responses to questions they've just heard or to gain courage to share what God is stirring in their hearts.

**INPUT IS AFFIRMED AND FOLLOWED UP.** Make sure you point out something true or helpful in a response. Don't just move on. Build community with follow-up questions, asking how other people have experienced similar things or how a truth has shaped their understanding of God and the Scripture you're studying. People are less likely to speak up if they fear that you don't actually want to hear their answers or that you're looking for only a certain answer.

**GOD AND HIS WORD ARE CENTRAL.** Opinions and experiences can be helpful, but God has given us the truth. Trust God's Word to be the authority and God's Spirit to work in people's lives. You can't change anyone, but God can. Continually point people to the Word and to active steps of faith.

# Additional Resources

Make your group aware of additional digital resources that are available through LifeWay.com/thechurchandtheracialdivide

**EBOOK.** In addition to the print book, this book is also available as an ebook which is immediately available after purchase in your LifeWay Reader library.

**ENHANCED EBOOK.** In addition to the ebook an enhanced ebook featuring integrated video assets such as a promotional video and session previews is also available after purchase in your LifeWay Reader library.

**DIGITAL VIDEO SESSIONS.** All six video teaching sessions are available to rent or purchase as individual, downloadable sessions. Additionally you will find a group use bundle that gives your church a license to share digital video content with multiple groups in your church.

# Session One

## Considerations

- Imago Dei is a Latin phrase meaning the image of God. This week is all about helping people understand what the image of God is and how that relates to the way we view other people.

- The core truth in the first session is this—all human beings are made in the image of God—everyone one of us, regardless of gender, race, age, ethnicity, or any other factor, reflects the goodness of God and exists to live in relationship with Him. Because of this truth, all people are of equal value and worth.

- There will be people in your group who have never heard this phrase before; there will be others still who have never see how this applies to the way we look at and view other people.

- Don't assume everyone understands what it means to be made in the image of God.

- Be patient with everyone, and make space for people to ask questions and seek clarification.

## Resources

### BOOKS

**The Dignity Revolution** by Daniel Darling. This book shows us how wonderful, liberating and empowering it is to be made in God's image and how this changes how we see ourselves and all other humans, and how we treat them and advocate for them.

**Restoring All Things** by Warren Cole Smith and John Stonestreet. Two leading experts on Christianity and culture cut through the chaos and uncertainty to show readers how God is powerfully active and intensely engaged in fulfilling his promise to restore all things unto himself.

### ARTICLE

**"What Does It Mean to be Made in the Image of God"** by David Clossum
erlc.com/resource-library/articles/what-does-it-mean-to-be-made-in-gods-image

# Session Two

## Considerations

- This week builds upon last week. Because all people are made in God's image.
- Connect God's mission to the nation to God's heart for all kinds of people to know Him.
- Give adequate time and space to discuss the practical suggestions Dr. Strickland makes at the close of teaching. Suggest people pursue these in groups or as a family for greater accountability.
- Help your group to see that part of the good work God gave us (Eph. 2:10) is to pursue relationships with people who don't look like you.

## Recommended Resources

### BOOKS

**The Book of Acts.** Read Acts looking for God's heart for all ethnicities. The leaders of the very first church to send missionaries to the world were from a diverse group of ethnicities and cultures.

*The Insanity of God* by Nik Ripken. Gain a sense of the specific ways God is at work in people groups that He loves around the world.

*Free at Last: The Gospel in the African-American Experience* by Carl F. Ellis Jr. Ellis Traces the gospel in the African-American experience from slavery through the end of the 20th century.

*Divided by Faith: Evangelical Religion and the Problem of Race in America* by Michael Emerson & Christian Smith. Research from nationwide surveys that can help you to see blind spots where your heart doesn't line up with God's heart for "all nations."

*Bloodlines* by John Piper. Sharing from his own experiences growing up in the segregated South, author John Piper thoughtfully exposes the ongoing problem of racism.

# Session Three

## Considerations

- More so than the last two sessions, this is where the rubber starts to meet the road. Take time to check in the group. See how they are being stretched and challenged. Consider doing this through individual texts, calls, or emails.
- People may get defensive when asked to consider their own apathy or ways they have exhibited partiality. This is meant to bring conviction, not confrontation. Pray for the Spirit to bring unity and peace to your group meeting.

## Resources

### BOOKS

*United: Captured by God's Vision for Diversity* by Trillia Newbell This book will inspire, challenge, and encourage readers to pursue the joys of diversity through stories of the author's own journey and a theology of diversity lived out.

*One Blood: Parting Words to the Church on Race and Love* by John Perkins. The final manifesto from a pioneer of racial reconciliation.

*Advocates: The Narrow Path to Racial Reconciliation* by Dhati Lewis. Using the book of Philemon, Lewis unpacks key principles that Paul applied to being an advocate in the midst of division.

### ARTICLES

**Preaching About Race: Keeping the Big Picture in View"** by David Prince. erlc.com/resource-library/articles/preaching-about-race-keeping-the-big-picture-in-view

**"Three Reasons White Pastors Need to Start Preaching on Race"** by Dan Darling factsandtrends.net/2015/06/26/three-reasons-white-pastors-need-to-start-preaching-on-race/

# Session Four

## *Considerations*

- This week's teaching is practical in ways that other weeks have not been. Press into that and encourage action.
- Recognize that some in your group with not actually have any relationships with people across ethnic lines. Don't make them feel bad about this, rather encourage them to seek diverse friendships.
- Maybe you, as the leader don't have diverse friendships, first think about what steps you could take here.
- Consider serving cross-culturally this week if your schedules allow.

## *Resources*

### BOOKS

*Building a Healthy Multi-ethnic Church* by Mark DeYmaz. This work illustrates both the biblical mandate for the multi-ethnic church as well as the seven core commitments required to bring it about.

### ARTICLES

**"Celebrating Multiethnic Churches"** by Jonathan Williams
imb.org/2019/04/11/celebrating-multi-ethnic-churches/

### CONFERENCE MESSAGES

View archived messages from the MLK 50 Conference hosted by the Gospel Coalition and the ERLC. www.thegospelcoalition.org/conference/mlk50/

# Session Five

## Considerations

- This week aims to established that sin is both personal and communal. This may be the first time that some in your group have every thought of societal justice.
- A holistic understanding of justice is the standard that God expects in our personal lives, our corporate lives together as the church, and in communities and social and political institutions.
- Try and keep people on topic and listening to the message as this session is likely to provide more opportunities for getting off-topic than other sessions.
- People may have hesitation in thinking of justice in systemic or societal terms, but all that is meant is seeking the wellness of a whole community.
- Because entire communities can experience injustice, we should also pursue justice in community.

## Resources

### PODCASTS

Phil Vischer Show podcast episode 267: "Race in America."
Phil Vischer talks with Skye Jethani and Christian Taylor about the statistics on systemic racism.
https://philvischer.com/the-phil-vischer-podcast/episode-267-race-in-america/

### BOOKS

*Just Mercy* by Bryan Stevenson. The lawyer who started the Equal Justice Initiative tells his story and many others of injustice in the legal system.

### VIDEOS

"We Need to Talk about an Injustice"- Bryan Stevenson
TED talk https://eji.org/videos/bryan-stevenson-ted-talk

*Leader Guide*

# Session Six

## Considerations

- The point of this session is to discover next steps. We cannot allow the fruit of our time together looking at race to translate into inaction.
- Use the following steps from our personal study to guide people towards action.

  1. Listen and Lament
  2. Confess and Repent
  3. Pray and Practice God's Presence
  4. Be Proximate to Suffering, Use your Position, and Expect Opposition

## Resources

### BOOKS

*The Warmth of Other Suns* by Isabella Wilkerson. A Pulitzer Prize-winning author chronicles one of the great untold stories of American history: the decades-long migration of black citizens who fled the South for northern and western cities, in search of a better life.

*The Gospel and Racial Reconciliation* edited by Russell Moore and Andrew Walker The Ethics and Religious Liberty Commission assemble leading voices to frame the issues with a gospel-centered perspective.

# WHERE TO GO FROM HERE

See how the gospel compels followers of Christ to counter culture on a wide variety of social issues in the world around them. (6 sessions)

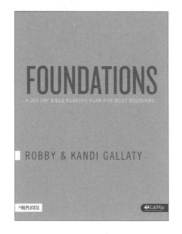

Read through the key, foundational passages of the Bible in one year with this five-days-per-week reading plan.

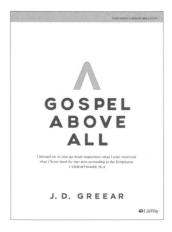

Discover that the impetus for the church's ministry is not a new strategy or an updated message but a return to elevating the gospel above all. (8 sessions)

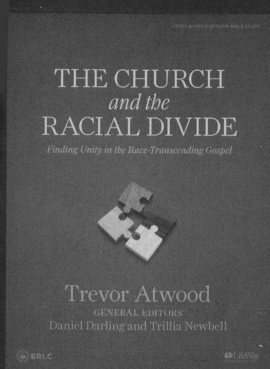

We hope you enjoyed *The Church and the Racial Divide*. Now that you've completed this study, here are some other possible options for your next one—from some of the contributors to this one.

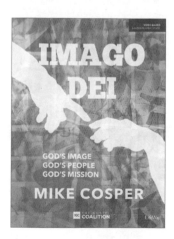

Learn how to view the image of God in three different ways: biblically, relationally, and missionally. (6 sessions)

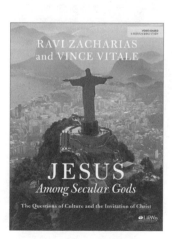

Learn how to confront the empty promises of cultural philosophies and develop confidence sharing the hope of Christ. (6 sessions)

Learn to reclaim the distinctiveness of the Christian faith that sets it apart from the surrounding culture. (6 sessions)

# WHAT HAPPENS WHEN YOU SEE EVERYTHING IN THE LIGHT OF THE GOSPEL?

It's that moment when you realize your heart cannot begin to hold all the love Jesus has for you. When you realize that moralism is empty and all of life is really about His life, death, and resurrection.

This new Bible study series will lead you on a one-year journey through the entire storyline of Scripture, showing how Jesus is the Hero from beginning to end.

When the light of the gospel transforms just one individual, it has the power to illuminate your group, your church, and even your entire community.

**GOSPEL**
**FOUNDATIONS**